CW01023669

GET REAL
GOD !
2

GET REAL GOD! 2

BIBLE STUDIES WITH ATTITUDE

MICHAEL FORSTER
DAVID GATWARD

First published in 2000 by
KEVIN MAYHEW LTD
Buxhall
Stowmarket
Suffolk IP14 3BW

© 2000 Michael Forster and David Gatward

The right of Michael Forster and David Gatward to be
identified as the authors of this work has been asserted
by them in accordance with the Copyright,
Designs and Patents Act 1988.

All rights reserved.
No part of this publication may
be reproduced, stored in a retrieval system,
or transmitted, in any form or by any means,
electronic, mechanical, photocopying, recording
or otherwise, without the prior written
permission of the publisher.

0 1 2 3 4 5 6 7 8 9

ISBN 1 84003 525 0
Catalogue No 1500346

Front cover designed by Jonathan Stroulger
Edited and typeset by Margaret Lambeth
Printed and bound in Great Britain

Contents

For-word

Forster and Gatward?
Gilbert and Sullivan?
Morecambe and Wise?
Chalk and cheese!
I knew there was a parallel somewhere.

What happens when an incredibly talented writer of Bible stories, with penetrating theological insight and unerring literary judgement allied to the wisdom of late middle age, pairs up with a brilliant, fresh young writer with a talent for composing simple yet profound prayers for teenagers?

No, I don't know, either – but if it ever happens it'll be terrific.

Enough of this dreaming. There are Bible study books and there are Bible study books. And there's this. I don't know what you're going to get out of it, but I hope it'll be something helpful.

As usual, Gatward has written the prayers in his unique, inimitable style (I tried to stop him, but he would insist) – as he does everything, of course.

Anyway, we reckon this is another interesting slant on telling Bible stories and you might just find some deep, profound meaning in it – in which case, write to us at KM, please, because we're still searching for it.

Oh, what the heck – enjoy.

MICHAEL FORSTER

Gat-word

Chalk and Cheese? Hmmm . . . maybe.

But whatever you call it, this book has been written by a youngish bloke (me) and an oldish bloke (him).

For some reason we manage to get on and have managed to create this rather tremendous book – for you.

Now don't go thinking it's great literature or that it's full of answers and will change your life. Some people think even the Bible is fallible, so what chance have we got? None. Exactly. But what it is (hopefully), is a load of stuff you'll enjoy, that'll get you thinking, and help you explore your beliefs and what they mean. It may challenge you too.

So read on, chill out, and don't take it with you on the bus – not that it's embarrassing, it's just a fairly big book to slip into your pocket.

DAVE G

Oh, Brother!

Based on Genesis 4:1-16

THINKING BIT

I'm quite prepared to concede that, when it comes to business, a bit of fair competition is a healthy thing – stops monopolies getting too much power and gives the consumer a modicum of protection. Mind you, even there it can lead to some pretty ghastly practices, but on the whole it's probably okay.

When it comes to faith and spirituality, though, competitiveness is as desirable as a box of matches in a kindergarten. And talking of kindergartens ...

READING BIT

The trouble with some people is they can't hack competition. Not that they particularly want to be successful themselves, mind you – they just don't want anyone else to do any better. That's how it was with Cain, who was one of Adam and Eve's sons. The other son, Cain's brother, was called Abel – and we'll have no silly jokes about things he was 'abel' to do, if you don't mind.

Cain and Abel had never really got on – fought like you wouldn't believe – and Eve got very anxious about it. 'I worry about those two,' she said to Adam. 'One day, one of them's going to get really hurt during their arguments.'

'Oh, don't exaggerate!' Adam replied. 'Boys will be boys, you know. Typical of a woman to get neurotic about it.'

Eve decided it wasn't worth dignifying that crack with an answer – which was really unfortunate, because Adam thought that he'd won, and from then on he had a feeling of superiority. Eve was right about Cain and Abel, though: one of them was about to get very badly hurt – like, permanently.

The real trouble started when both brothers decided to give something to God. Abel's job was to look after the livestock –

sheep, goats, cattle, that kind of thing – so he decided to give God a lamb as a gift. When you see the tradition he started, it's probably a good thing he didn't decide to give him a pig, or a goat, or – well, perhaps we'd better get on with the story.

Cain was at a bit of a loss. 'Can't have God thinking I don't love him,' he thought, 'but how can I compete with that?' Cain didn't have any animals – the only livestock he had anything to do with were living in his hair, and he didn't think God wanted one of those. Well, he decided, if his offering couldn't be better, it'd just have to be bigger. So it was that, just as Abel was making his offering to God, Cain staggered up with a huge barrow-load of fruit and veg. 'There you are, God,' he puffed as he tipped out the whole lot on the ground with a crash that turned Abel's lambs into woolly jumpers, 'now, that's what I call an offering.'

God wasn't impressed. I mean, he seriously wasn't impressed. 'Have you got compost where your brain should be?' he asked. '(That'll teach you to wash you hands before meals.) Look, I don't need this stuff, but at least Abel had good motives – you were just trying to get one up on him. So why don't you just fertilise your fruit trees and leave me to enjoy Abel's lamb? Any mint sauce anywhere?'

Well, I've known some spoilt brats, but Cain must have been practising. He'd probably have won an Oscar, except that in the Stone Age bronze was a bit on the scarce side. Tears, screams, stamping, it was all very impressive – perhaps a tad uncoordinated, and lacking polish, but then he hadn't been to Wimbledon to watch the experts. The printable bit was something about getting even with Abel.

As murders go it was a bit primitive, but not bad for a first attempt. The only trouble was, Cain hadn't really taken on board the permanence of it all. Abel wasn't just going to get up and walk away – that only happens on TV, and Eve couldn't afford the licence. So there he was with a dead brother and a live issue: what could he tell the family? While he was thinking about it, God broke into his thoughts.

'Hello, Cain – where's Abel?'

Well, what do you say, when you've just topped your brother

and God asks where he is? Cain could have said, 'Well, if you don't know, who does?' but he really wasn't that bright – or that brave. So he just said, 'Am I his keeper or something?'

'Keeper? Keeper? Why would Abel want a keeper?' God replied. 'Mind you, a brother would be good.'

'I'm his brother,' said Cain, without stopping to think.

'Really?' rejoined God. 'Then it can't have been you that killed him, because brothers don't do that sort of thing.'

'Oh, so you know then.'

'Gosh, Cain, did you think of that all by yourself? Yes, I most certainly do know. Now, even you can't be daft enough to think you can just go home as though nothing's happened?'

'I can't go *anywhere*,' Cain protested. 'If people know what I've done, they'll kill me.'

'Oh, no!' God answered. 'You don't get off the hook that easily – you've got to live with what you've done. You're going to be a marked man for the rest of your life, rejected by everybody and with only your conscience for company.'

What a prospect! Abel might have been a pain in the neck, but at least he hadn't been around all the time. But where do you go to get away from your conscience?

PRAYING BIT

Lord,
I'm not much good when it comes to competition,
    especially at school.
I've lost every running race,
    failed a few exams
    and never been picked for a team.
My life seems to be one continuous last place.

I sound low, don't I, Lord?
Don't mean to be.
And at least I haven't hired any hitmen
    to take out those who keep beating me.
You see, I understand why there's competition,
    it's just that it doesn't sit well with me
    and who I am.
I even lose when I'm racing myself.
How sad is that?

Life seems to be one massive competition.
Everyone against everyone else,
    trying to do better,
    get better results,
    earn more money.
But the trouble with competition
    is that there are always those who keep winning,
    and those of us who keep losing.
It doesn't seem very fair.

I think you've caught me at a bad time, Lord.
I'm sorry.
I'd just like to know that perhaps, one day,
    I'll get to the finishing line
    and you'll be there waiting.

Amen.

The Lion's Tale

Based on Genesis 6-8

THINKING BIT

'Remnant theology': no matter how great the disaster, God always manages to do something with whatever's left over. Clever stuff, eh?

READING BIT

Hi, there – Lionel's the name, and I'm the mane man around here, if you get my drift. Actually, I haven't been well for a day or two, all because I ate something that disagreed with me – a bumptious little zebra who kept rattling on about someone he called 'God' and telling me I'd got to change my ways. I wasn't being told to change anything by a creature with *his* dress sense. 'Repent!' he kept yelling at me. 'Repent, or you shall surely die!' Well, he got part of it right. I didn't repent, but he died. Perhaps I wouldn't have got ill if I'd taken his pyjamas off before I swallowed him.

Anyway, I was going to tell you about how I came to be cooped up on a boat, surrounded by food on the hoof and not allowed to eat any of it.

It all started with this man called Noah. He was into this 'God' thing, as well, and he reckoned he'd had a message saying the earth was going to be destroyed by a flood. He had the idea of taking two of everything that lived onto a boat, to ride out the storm, and start things off again afterwards.

Of course, I knew the old sea-dog was barking, but Petal (that's the wife) said we should go along with it. 'You never know,' she purred, 'there just might be something in it.' That's the last thing I needed – a woman with an opinion – but then she said something that appealed to my better nature. 'Just think – sharing a boat with all that live meat.'

Now, that made sense. So we went along. We'd been watching Noah build his boat for some time, and he certainly made a good job of it. So we packed our bags and joined the queue to embark.

When we got on board, we were shown to our cabin – a bit basic, but as we weren't paying what could we expect? I only realised later that it wasn't a cabin, it was a cage. Of course, it was all Petal's fault – women are supposed to think of these things, aren't they! So there we were, surrounded by fresh meat and being fed by humans on convenience food. It's bad enough eating freeze-dried skunk, even when it's not past its sell-by date. The hyenas in the next cage thought it was a huge joke, and spent the entire voyage giggling like silly school-cubs.

Give Noah his due, though, he was right – and so was Petal, but I'd eat my own mane before I'd admit it to her. You never saw rain like it! Forty solid days of it – and St Swithin hadn't even been thought of then, so who do you blame? Noah was still rabbiting on about God wanting to clean the world up and start afresh. So that's why he wanted two of everything – but did he have to include the fleas? Nasty, small-minded creatures, fleas (small everything, I suppose, really) – you'd be amazed how much backbiting can go on in a small community. Why can't we all just learn to get along together, is what I want to know. I'd be very happy to live in peace with my neighbours – as long as I wasn't hungry, that is. Mind you, the hyenas would have to grow up a bit.

Once the rain stopped, life wasn't too bad at first – the sun came out, and there was nothing to do but lie and enjoy it. I even began to think that freeze-dried skunk might be a price worth paying. It got a bit of a bore, though, and my beautiful coat lost all its gloss. Now you may say it's a sin, but a lion must have his pride – and mine was down to two, including me.

And things got worse – the rations started to get low, and we found we were eating things we wouldn't even have given the time of day to in any other circumstances. 'Is it worth it?' I asked. 'I mean, will posterity ever appreciate what we put up with just so they could have a life?' Petal said that wasn't the point – it was all about something she called 'remnant theology'. I said I knew all about remnants – that was all we'd been eating for months.

Anyway, things did eventually get better. One of the doves

went out for a recce and came back with an olive leaf in its beak. Well, you never saw such an undignified scrabble for a morsel of food. Noah saw the point, though – it meant the tree-tops were showing, so the water was going down. Not before time, either – if I had to spend one more day than necessary being looked down on and sneered at by those giraffes I think I'd have gone even pottier than Noah. Eventually, the dove took off and didn't come back, which seemed to suggest there was some land showing as well, so we'd soon be back on terra firma. And talking of terror, those chimps had better keep out of my way or they'd find out that life in the jungle ain't no tea party.

Crrrrunchhh! Trust Noah to go and run aground! If he'd been more careful we could have let the waters go down some more, and then settled on a nice flat plain, but no – right up on the top of a mountain with not a rope or a crampon between us. And humans think they're so superior! I was just saying to Petal that I hoped this 'God' character wasn't going to make a habit of floods like this, when these lights appeared before my eyes. The concussion must have been worse than I thought – great arcs of light across the sky, and then this eerie, dis-embodied voice: 'That's my rainbow, Noah – my sign of hope. It's a new beginning, and the world will never be destroyed by water again.'

Hallucinations, voices . . . that's what happens when you don't have enough fresh meat in your diet.

PRAYING BIT

So, Lord,
    you can do anything with anything
    no matter how messy it is?
Excellent!
Well, it makes me feel a little better, anyway.

I'm the human equivalent of a well-used compost heap –
lots of rubbish and a bit smelly.
But you reckon you can see the good in me,
    and from all of this
    you can create something great.

From me?
How is that possible?
I'm a bad Christian.
I question everything.
I do most things wrong.
I'm stubborn.

Do you really mean it, Lord?
That from me,
    little manky me,
    something good will come?
I hope so.
I don't want to be a waste.

Use the compost of me, Lord,
    and grow something beautiful.

Amen.

Promises, Promises . . .

Based on Genesis 12:1-21:3

THINKING BIT

God seems to choose the most unlikely people – almost makes you wonder at times whether he really knows what he's doing. I certainly wouldn't have chosen Abraham for what God had in mind, but then I'm not God – which is really rather a good thing for all concerned.

READING BIT

I don't know whether I'm allowed to say 'gobsmacked' in a book of religious stories, but if I'm not then I'm not going to be able to tell you how I think Abraham probably felt when God told him he was going to be a father.

'Well, goodness me!' he expostulated. 'I'm terribly amazed.'

'No, you're not,' God corrected him, 'you're gobsmacked. But that word won't be invented for about 4000 years – and even then, some religious people might not like it – so you'd better stick with "terribly amazed".'

And so it was. But why, you ask, was Abraham so terribly amazed? Probably because he was coming up for his telegram from the Queen (except that, like 'gobsmacked', they hadn't been invented yet, either – telegrams, that is, not queens). Now, if fertility in senility seems to have more rhyme than reason about it, bear in mind that Sarah wasn't much younger: pushing ninety, in fact – and that was the only kind of pushing she had any inclination to do.

And that wasn't all. God seemed to have it in mind for them to move house – something most experts might think best left until the sprog can at least walk by itself, if not carry its own luggage, but God thought differently. 'Get going,' he said. 'I'm going to give you a new country of your own, and use you to start an entirely new nation.'

So they set off – without knowing where they were going, how they were going to live or what sort of neighbours they were going to have when they arrived. Hardly the sort of thing that your average young couple with prospects, pension schemes and a fixed-rate mortgage would do nowadays – but Abraham and Sarah were lucky not to have any of those problems to hold them back.

Seemed a bit strange, though – especially as Sarah didn't show any signs of actually getting pregnant. 'I hope God will get a move on,' she said one day. 'We're not getting any younger, you know.' (Why do people say that? I mean, it's hardly a devastatingly original insight, is it?)

Anyway, to continue: I won't tell you the whole story, because it goes on for ages. It has its moments, though – let's just say it's a good thing you don't have to be good to be important to God, because these two got up to some distinctly dodgy goings on along the way. Of course, they said they were just trying to help God out. Yeah, yeah, we've heard that one before – and from better philosophers than them, as well.

So there they were, journeying on like a couple of old-age New Age travellers, when they had a Visitation. A couple of angels called in for tea one day. They didn't look like angels, but that's the way God works. If it comes to that, Abraham didn't look much like a young stud about to father an entire nation, but we've noted that already. Anyway, thinking they were just another couple of travellers, Abraham sat under a tree with them and shared some food, by way of being civil. During the conversation, one of the strangers said, 'Where's your wife?'

'Oh, she's in the tent,' said Abraham, not realising that Sarah had come to the tent doorway to listen.

'Well,' said the man, 'I'll visit you again in a year and you can show me your new baby.'

Funny thing to say, with Sarah looking about as pregnant as your average lightweight ironing board – and Sarah certainly did think it was funny.

'Why did your wife laugh?' asked one of the visitors.

Sarah covered up: 'Laugh? Why should I laugh? What have I got to laugh about, slaving away in a hot tent while you fellas scoff all the food?'

'Oh, yes,' the visitor insisted. 'You laughed.' And the two men got up and went away, thanking Abraham for his hospitality.

'No trouble at all,' Abraham assured them grandly, as Sarah gathered up the dirty plates and cups and went into the tent to eat the leftovers. She'd never realised until then that she was developing a bit of a craving for date-and-cucumber sandwiches. Why had she never realised before how nice they were, she wondered, as she spooned some custard onto a bowl of roast potatoes for her pudding.

Abraham came in and saw her. 'You're mad!' he said. 'Either that, or pregnant.'

'Oh, don't you start!' Sarah shouted, and Abraham ducked the flying saucer and went outside, roaring with laughter.

Things didn't get any better: asking for strawberries with beef dripping wouldn't have been so unreasonable if the strawberries had been in season, but when Sarah started asking for pomegranates in mustard-and-mint sauce, Abraham knew it was serious: Sarah was seriously pregnant.

They called the baby boy Isaac. Passing tradespeople wondered why they hadn't chosen a more ordinary name – like Shamus O'Flaherty MacNamara, for example – but Abraham thought that sounded a bit conventional and boring.

'It's going to be Isaac,' he said firmly.

So that's what they called him.

And it stuck – which is what happens when you call people names.

Get Real, God! 2

PRAYING BIT

So, Lord,
   why do you choose such unlikely people?
I'm not just talking about Abraham and Sarah.
What about the disciples?
Or Jonah?

Or me?

I'm weird, Lord,
   very strange;
   hardly 'disciple' material.
I'm picky, annoying, angry, sad, happy, low, fussy,
   desperate, lonely, unsure, unconvinced, critical, crazy
   and obsessed with shoes.
So why did you pick me?

And, while we're on the subject of being 'picked',
   what have I been picked for?
Why won't you tell me?
I'm floating along,
   getting through life,
   not knowing what to do,
   where to go.
And you say you've chosen me!
That you have a purpose for me!
How insane does that sound?
Very.

Just let me in on the plan at some point, OK?
Thanks.

Amen.

20

Subversive Hope

Based on Exodus 2:1-10

THINKING BIT

Call God subversive, and pillars of the establishment start
shaking with indignation. But what else do you say of a God
who creates hope, and enables it to grow right at the heart of
unjust systems?

From Moses to Jesus, and on to Martin Luther King Jr and
Nelson Mandela, God brings hope to birth and fosters it at the
very heart of pain and despair. Well that's definately better than a
poke in the eye with a sharp rejoiner.

READING BIT

PRINCESS HAS SECRET BABY

Gossip columnist Tootin' Carmen investigates a potential scandal in Pharaoh's palace:

Only *Mummy's Weekly* can bring you this kind of story,
because only *Mummy's Weekly*, as an underground publication, is not bound by official press releases. And now, at great
personal risk to ourselves, we break the scandal of the century.

Rumours have been circulating for some time of a dark
secret in Pharaoh's household, so I decided to go undercover,
posing as a freelance masseuse, to beat a path to the truth.
Risking all for the public interest, I penetrated to the heart of the
royal family itself, and there found the cause of all the gossip.

Baby
Now I can reveal the stunning truth that Princess Ramasa has a
baby. 'Whose is it?' is the next question. Calculating from the
age of the infant, it certainly isn't the prince's – he was away on
a goodwill visit to Ethiopia at the vital moment. So I began to

ferret around, and the story just got better and better.

The word of a reliable source (who must remain anonymous since she's grown attached to her head and prefers it to stay where the gods put it) is that this is no love child of some palace servant – in fact it's not even Egyptian at all. This is the child of – wait for it – a Hebrew slave. Now, I'd like to be able to give you a nice, juicy, *Sultry Sex with Slave on Sand-dune* story, but it's even better than that.

Found

My reliable source, an eye-witness to the whole event, claimed that the baby was found in a basket, floating among the reeds at the edge of the Nile. My curiosity now fully aroused, I pursued the story, careless of my own safety and concerned only for the truth and my valued readers.

And now, I can reveal all.

It seems that the baby was born to a Hebrew slave family. Seeing that it was a boy, they knew they should kill it under the new Slave Population Control Act. But this family is made of sterner stuff than that, and looked for a way to save it. The resourceful mother hit on the idea of a basket, made from reeds and waterproofed with tar, cunningly concealed among the bulrushes on the edge of the Nile. But this courageous family had reckoned without the baby's powerful lungs. His pitiful cries attracted the attention of some bathers, among whom was none other than Princess Ramasa herself.

My source told me that the baby's sister was keeping watch nearby and saw the whole incident. So I set off on the trail of the mystery sister who must remain anonymous, and will be referred to as 'Miss M'.

Really, really

Miss M told me, 'I was on the bank, keeping watch, and of course I was horrified when the princess came to bathe and found the baby. But she seemed really, really nice, so I went and spoke to her. She obviously really, really liked the baby – she called him "Moses" because he came out of the water – but she didn't know how to look after him. I told her I knew someone who'd make an ace nurse, and I'd be really, really pleased to go and get her.'

In the interests of security, I am unable to confirm the identity of the nurse she found, but you all know how strongly I believe that a child should be reared, wherever possible, by the natural mother. I can now report that this child is safe and well, and being brought up in the palace in the best possible way.

Our Political Correspondent adds:

These are dangerous times, and political speculation is a risky enough business, even without mixing it with religion. But even so, it is hard not to see the hand of the Israelite slaves' God in this. The presence so close to the seat of power of a male Israelite must be unsettling for the current administration. As the child grows to maturity, it will be interesting to see where the divided loyalties eventually lead him.

Can the dated and uncivilised institution of slavery survive a subversive presence such as this?

Tootin' Carmen adds:

Oh, get lost, you pontificating old windbag. Go and find another story to spoil.

PRAYING BIT

I read the Bible, Lord
   (I do! Honest!),
   and I get the sense that
   woven into all the stories
   is a tremendous amount of theatrics.
That's not me being rude, Lord.
I love it!
All those unlikely heroes
   plucked from obscurity;
   all those really bad baddies.
It's great!

And all that subversive stuff –
   lots of toppling of pillars,
   and upsetting people who think they're important.
So much hope and strength
   coming from people who seem to be so 'normal',
   so full of insecurities, questions, problems.

People like me . . .

And that makes me think, Lord.
You used these people,
   like Moses,
   and moved mountains,
   often in spite of them.

Could you do the same with me, Lord?

Amen.

A Reluctant Hero

Based on Exodus 3:1-4:17

THINKING BIT

During the Salvadoran civil war, someone asked a freedom fighter what he wanted to do after the war was over. If they expected some grandiose plan for high governmental office, they were sadly let down. 'I want to go back to my farm,' he said, 'and rear chickens.' Hardly the stereotypical idea of an ambitious political firebrand!

You don't need to be 'interested in politics' to be a liberator of people: just concerned about justice.

READING BIT

Now, I ask you – did I ever apply for this job? I was perfectly happy as a shepherd, working for my father-in-law Jethro, keeping my nose clean and the sheep well fed. As far as politics was concerned, I'd had a brush with that a few years before – killed an Egyptian slave driver who was beating a slave – and what thanks did I get for it? None. None of them backed me up. Quite the contrary – one of them threw it back in my face when I tried to help him. That's when I knew I had to get out, so I came here. It's safe, quiet, and I feel appreciated.

Still, I might have got out of Egypt but I can't get Egypt out of me. I was born a Hebrew. Yes, I grew up in Pharaoh's palace with all the privileges that entails, but somehow I always knew I was really a Hebrew. When I finally found out it was true, it was devastating. Still, I tried to help them and look what I got – nothing. So why should I care any more? A shepherd's life for me from now on.

Most of the time I managed to forget about it – I've got a great family, and believe it or not, sheep are really interesting creatures – but I suppose I always knew that I couldn't ignore the call for ever. From time to time, one of the farm workers would come back from a business trip to Egypt with stories about how lousy the slaves' lives were, and I just had this nagging feeling that I should be doing something.

Then it happened. It was just an ordinary day, and I was out looking for fresh pasture for the sheep when this bush just burst into flame. Honestly – spontaneous combustion I suppose, but it wasn't quite that simple. The bush was burning furiously, but the leaves stayed green – the fire seemed to burn the bush without actually destroying it. Now that's not like any kind of fire I've come across before, so I naturally wanted to see a bit more and went closer.

'And just where do you think you're going with those shoes?'

'Eh? Who was that? And what's wrong with my shoes, anyway?'

'Nothing, but where are your manners?'

By now I was just about ready to run, but that bush really fascinated me and I just couldn't turn my back on it. Could it be the voice was actually coming from there? Now I knew I was in trouble. Talking to bushes might be horticulture, but listening to them is definitely psychosis.

'Get a grip, Moses – you know you aren't supposed to wear shoes on holy ground. Now get them off.'

You've got to remember we hadn't exactly had a lot to do with God for quite a while. We sort of knew he was there, and we remembered some folk tales about the past, but when you're an unpaid overworked shepherd, or brickie with targets to meet, you don't tend to spend much time thinking deeply and meaningfully about philosophy. So we'd sort of lost contact with all the religious stuff. Why did I get the feeling that was about to change? I took my shoes off – it seemed easier than arguing about it – and then I went forward for a closer look. But I still couldn't see anybody – just that weird fire and the curious, disembodied voice.

'Right, Moses – now listen, and listen good.'

I nearly said, 'You mean "listen well",' but I remembered who I was talking to, so I just said, 'Certainly your Excellen – your Worsh – look, just what am I supposed to call you?'

'All in good time,' said the Voice. 'For now, just listen. I've been seeing what's going on in Egypt and I'm not impressed.'

'No, I know,' I said, 'but they're working as hard as they can – and if Pharaoh got some straw supplies . . .'

'I told you to listen,' the Voice cut in. 'I'm talking about the way the Hebrews are being treated. I'd have thought you could hear their screams for help from here – or have I got to invent television before anybody takes any notice?'

I decided to listen – whatever television was, I had a feeling it was better not invented until absolutely unavoidable.

'It's time to set my people free,' said the Voice. 'You're to go to Pharaoh and tell him that I demand my people's freedom.'

Fine, I thought: 'Oh, and while I'm here, Pharaoh old bean, did you want to talk about that dead slave driver?' I think not.

'Look, God, or Elohim, or whoever you are – you don't want me. I can't speak for toffee – can't string three words together. No you need someone really impressive what can talk right.' Somehow, that didn't sound as convincing as I had intended.

'Not convincing,' came the reply. 'I'll be with you all the way.'

I tried a different tack. 'Look, you have to face the reality, you know. No one remembers who you are – I'd almost forgotten, myself. They're going to want to know a bit more about you than a strange voice coming from a pyrotechnical bush. So just who are you?'

'Don't come all that Jeremy Paxman stuff with me,' came the reply. (Jeremy who??) 'Labels are for things – I'm beyond definition. *I* decide who and what I am, and I'm not about to have some jumped-up philosopher narrowing me down with human categories.'

By now I was completely lost, and the Voice seemed to sense it. It softened slightly. 'Look, you're not going to be alone. I'll be there. And if you really don't feel confident to do the talking, take you brother Aaron with you. He can talk.'

That's true. He can talk the hind leg off a Bactrian camel, can Aaron. Mind you, this Voice was doing pretty well for someone with no visible mouth. I decided to stop arguing and give it a go – and that was the start of the greatest story you're ever likely to hear. But you'll have to read it elsewhere because I've got a nation to liberate. See you.

PRAYING BIT

A lot of things annoy me, Lord,
   and I know you know that.
But I need to say it.
I'm not talking small things here either,
   like the usual list I bring
   of homework, relationships, spots,
   and scabby knees.
I'm talking 'biggies',
   like homelessness,
   war,
   famine,
   abuse,
   loneliness,
   racism,
   sexism,
   bigotry,
   ignorance,
   discrimination,
   bullying . . .

And that's just the tip of the iceberg, Lord.

Such a long list of pain
   for such a beautiful world.
It's so sad, Lord,
   so unnecessary.
And I feel so small
   when I think, 'How can I make a difference?'
Because I don't feel that I can.

Help me, Lord,
   to bring in the changes.

Amen.

Tunnelling Through the Sea

Based on Exodus 14

THINKING BIT

Freedom's great in theory but sometimes a bit grim in reality. You've got to make decisions, live with the consequences, learn to get along with others who are also 'free' but different – all kinds of stuff. Sometimes we have hard choices – not between good and bad but between bad and worse, which might not be so tough if we knew which was which.

READING BIT

Don't talk to me about liberation! Moses had got us out of Egypt with a whole lot of talk about 'freedom' and a 'Promised Land', but he hadn't told us there was a great big desert between us and this wondrous destination. We didn't mind too much, at first – anything was better than building Pharaoh's lousy monument, especially with home-made bricks. But then the down-side hit us: baking hot by day when we were travelling, and freezing cold at night when we wanted to sleep – and the most mind-boggling creepy-crawlies you could ever imagine. 'Archibald,' I said to myself, 'this ain't going to be no picnic outing.'

Things improved when we camped at the seaside. Well, the kids loved it, of course, and I saw distinct commercial possibilities: we could open the world's first holiday camp and charge people a fortune to stay. There'd be a huge demand from exhausted, stressed-out Egyptians trying to manage without slaves for the first time, and we could get our own back by making them play embarrassing games in the ballroom. Then just as I was putting my business plan together to take to the money lender, I saw this huge cloud of dust on the horizon. Just my luck – visitors, and we hadn't even begun to build a single chalet block.

Just as I was starting on some plans for temporary emergency accommodation, one of the lookouts came rushing into the camp shouting, 'Egyptians! The Egyptians are coming!' That could only mean one thing – they'd got fed up with doing their own ironing and sent the army to bring us back. Well, I didn't wait for anyone else, or stop to pack my family heirlooms (a toothpick and a lucky mummified nail-clipping said to be Joseph's). I just turned and ran – straight into the sea!

Trust Moses!

'Freedom,' he called it. 'Rats in a trap,' I called it. Stuck between Pharaoh and the deep blue sea, and I wasn't sure which was worse. Then I realised we should never have come. Slavery hadn't been that bad. Okay, so they brutalised us regularly and did what they wanted with our women; the hours were a touch unsocial and the pay non-existent – but at least we got fed and housed. You could bet they wouldn't be as nice to us after they'd had to come out into this rotten desert to get us back. That's it, we should never have come. And it was all Moses' fault. Well, it wasn't mine – nothing was ever my fault.

'Call yourself a leader,' I yelled at him. 'Weren't the graves in Egypt good enough for you, you over-inflated ego on legs? I told you this would happen – told you we were better off staying in Egypt – but would you listen? No! You had to drag us out here, against our will, taking advantage of our self-doubt and lack of "personhood" . . .' (nothing like a bit of anachronistic jargon to put someone in their place) '. . . and then get us either drowned or dissected out here in the desert. Well, thanks a bunch, Moses – remind me never again to listen to you.'

I won't tell you what Moses said to me, because I don't think it was very polite – and certainly not an appropriate response to my restrained language. But then he called all the people together and did a kind of 'broadcast to the nation'.

'Don't be afraid,' he said. 'Stand your ground,' he said. Oh, sure – and Pharaoh about to give his armaments manufacturers a field day. 'Just stay firm, and watch God deal with the Egyptians,' he said.

'God' again! Wouldn't this guy ever grow up? Didn't he know that 'God' was just a way unenlightened people used to talk – just a metaphor for goodness and a convenient explanation for happy coincidences? I mean, what age was he living in, for God's – sorry, goodness' sake? But everyone else seemed to be going along with this, so I didn't have much choice, did I?

'I give it until morning,' I told my wives. 'Then we'll see who's right – and when Moses is lying dead, with his head severed, then he'll wish he'd listened to me!'

So we went to bed – all except Moses, who spent the night standing with his staff stretched out over the sea, looking like some kind of anthropomorphic signpost. Utterly mad! That night no one slept a wink, though, anyway. This howling east wind really whipped up the sea into a frenzy. 'Great!' I thought. 'That really finishes any chance of getting away.' So as soon as it was light, we got up and went outside – might as well enjoy our last sunrise. I couldn't believe what I saw.

The wind was still howling, and I could hear the sea, but at first I didn't see it. Then I realised: the wind had separated the water, which was piled up on either side leaving a wide, dry path through the middle.

'Well, don't just stand there gawping,' yelled Moses. 'Get going. I told you God would get us out.'

No! Seriously! He really wanted us to walk through that – with about 50 billion litres of water on each side and only this freak wind keeping it apart? We all know that the desert winds can drop as quickly as they start, and this one had been going all night already. I was about to say, 'Not on your cotton-picking life,' when I heard the sound of something even more terrifying – Egyptian horses' hooves. Oh, what the heck – we were going to die anyway, and at least this would deprive Pharaoh of the satisfaction.

So off we went – people, horses, wagons, the lot. Gradually we got toward the middle of the sea, and of course the walls of water were higher. The noise was terrifying, and we were just waiting for all that water to come crashing down. I wanted to run, but knew it would be useless – I'd only get exhausted, and collapse right there on the sea bed. So we just kept trudging on, seemingly for ever and ever. Then we realised we could see the other side, and we began to quicken our pace. I couldn't believe it when we actually arrived, and I must admit it felt good – even if we did have to put up with Moses and his silly sister singing and dancing and going on about 'God'. Didn't they know a freak of nature when they saw it? Mind you, it was uncanny how the water all closed up again after we'd got across but just in time to stop the Egyptians.

Looking back on it, I must admit I sometimes wonder; and just occasionally (when there's really no other way out) I do say a little prayer. But if ever you tell anybody . . .

PRAYING BIT

I can't define it, Lord,
   this 'freedom' thing.
In some ways I see myself as really free,
   because I am.
I'm in a position to control my future,
   to make something of myself.
I've got friends, family,
   and a social life.
I can choose what I want to do,
   when I want to.
So I'm fairly free, I can't deny it.

But occasionally, Lord,
I get a twinge inside,
   like a sense of panic,
   and I want to escape
   from this world,
   from where I am,
   from who I am.
I feel trapped,
   suffocated,
   shut up.

Am I ungrateful?
After all, so many millions are so less free than I am.
I'm lucky,
   but that doesn't make it any easier.

I'm sorry, Lord.
I just find it sad
   that in this 'free' world,
   with so much choice,
   so many of us feel trapped.

Free us all.

Amen.

Pop Goes the Idol

Based on Exodus 32:1-24

THINKING BIT

Why do people always want to be certain of everything? I mean, just think it through for a moment: no risk, no surprises, no discovery, no mystery, no room for growth.

Sounds like hell to me. Give me a desert journey, any time.

READING BIT

Look, okay, it was a mistake – do you really have to rub it in by making *me* tell the story? Can't you do it from someone else's point of view? I mean, have you any idea what it's like being Moses' brother? Whatever I did, I'd never actually been taken seriously for myself.

'Let me introduce Aaron – he's Moses' brother you know.'

'Yes, it's a good idea Aaron, but what does Moses think?'

'Does Moses know you were out until 3 a.m. yesterday?'

I tell you, I'm fed up with it – I want a life. I want to be valued for what I can give. So when I got the chance, can you blame me for taking it?

I'd never been able to understand why they idolised Moses so much, anyway – as far as I could see they'd had nothing but trouble ever since he put the frighteners on Pharaoh and led them to what he called 'freedom' – wall-to-wall sand, snakes, spiders and not a belly-dancer to be seen anywhere. Life was pretty tough, I don't mind telling you, and while we were slogging away to keep body and soul together, where was Moses? Helping dig for water? Hardly. Gathering firewood with a working party? Never. Taking a turn at sentry duty on the camp perimeter? Not on your life – that could be dangerous, of course.

So where was he? I'll tell you: up a mountain, communing with God.

Well, as I said to my friend Reuben, we could all do that,

couldn't we – cut ourselves off from real life and use God as the excuse – but some of us have to keep the world afloat. And you know what was worst? I just had the feeling that he was going to go down in history, and I was going to get the bit part again. Now d'you see why I was brassed off?

(Yes, alright, I'm getting there – I'm setting the scene – it's important. Don't you know anything about writing?)

Anyway, while Moses was up the pole – sorry, the mountain – I was taking all the flack.

'You're Moses' brother, aren't you? Do something.' They'd lost faith in this God that only Moses ever seemed to meet, and were fed up with taking his word about things.

'Okay,' I said, 'I'll give you a god you can see.' Well, by this time they were so desperate they'd have done anything, so when I passed the bag round they put in their gold earrings, bangles, ankle chains – all the gold they had, and I melted it down. Making the mould was easy – same principle as making bricks, but more creative – and then we poured in the liquid gold and made this bull-calf. Okay, so it wasn't particularly life-like, but who cares – it was visible – and it was ours.

'That's it,' I called out. 'A god you can see – and it's made from all the most precious things you had.'

'That's great,' said Reuben. 'Now we don't have to believe in things we can't see, anymore.' And before I knew it everyone was pressing round to touch the idol – something else they couldn't do with the God Moses was obsessed about.

I wrote a special prayer for our first worship service. 'O wonderful calf,' it went, 'we thank you for being small enough for us to see and understand. We praise you that now we no longer need to look beyond our own experience, or think about anything we don't already know. Thank you for being completely *our* god, and not shared with anyone else.' Then the choir leader taught us this special chorus he'd written for the occasion:

You're the god of our drea-ea-ea-eams.
Everything is just the way it see-ee-ee-eems;
nothing is a mystery any more,
you're the only wonderful, amazing god that we adore.

Ooh, ooh, ooh, ooh,
ooh, ooh, ooh, ooh,
ooh, ooh, ooh, ooh,
you're the only wonderful, amazing god that we adore.

To be honest, I was a bit dubious about the scan of that last line, but it was heaps better than most of the stuff the choir leader wrote, so I let it go.

Just as we were getting into our stride, someone called out, 'Here comes Moses!' and everyone scattered. 'Oh, right,' I thought. 'I was the main man around here until Big M condescended to pay us a visit, and all of a sudden they're all scared of him.' Oh, don't be crass – of course I was scared, too, but only because they'd all cleared off and left me to face him. They didn't deserve me.

Moses went ballistic. 'Who's responsible for this?' he bellowed, and as if in answer a trembling hand came round the side of a tent and pointed at me. I'd probably have known whose hand it was, if only I hadn't melted down everyone's rings, but you can't be wise after the event.

'What have you done?' roared my brother. Well, since I obviously wasn't going to get any backup from that miserable lot of cowards I did the only thing any sensible person would do. I grovelled.

'Well,' I said, 'it's the strangest thing – you'll laugh when you hear it. We lit this fire, and I put this gold on it, and – well, out popped this calf.' Well, *you* try to think of something better in a crisis like that. Moses didn't laugh, though.

'Right,' he said, 'so that's a god is it? That's the source of all goodness and wholeness – the very essence of life itself? Fine. Prove it.'

I didn't like the way things were going. 'Prove it?'

'Grind it down, sprinkle it on the drinking water, and swallow hard. If it's full of life you should feel wonderful afterwards.'

He made us do it, too. I've not been the same since. And the next person who offers me 'a drop of the hard stuff' is going to feel even worse.

PRAYING BIT

Plans, Lord,
   I'm supposed to be making plans.
I'm supposed to think about what I want to do,
   know where I want to be
   and plan my whole life . . . now.

I can't.
I don't want to.
I won't.

You see,
   it seems mad that the now me should know
   what the future me will want, and be, and enjoy, and do.
The now me wants adventure, excitement, the unknown . . .
   not this career-path + marriage + retirement.
(Whatever any of that actually is.)

Am I mad?
I guess so, but I can't decide,
   and I need to make certain people think that I can.
Does that make sense?

You've given me this life,
   this gift of such hugeness,
   and I don't want to sign it over
   to what everyone else thinks I should do with it.
It's not selfish, or unrealistic,
   it's just the way I am.

And you made me!

And I thank you for that, Lord.
Thank you that I want to do something with my life,
   to live it to the full,
   to squeeze every drop of adventure from it,
   and be able to say, 'Here you go, Lord. I did it.'

Amen.

Mixed Marriage

Based on The Book of Ruth

There's nothing new about prejudice, but God does seem to have a way of showing it up for the stupidity it is – that is if we pay attention to him, which your average intellectually challenged bigot probably doesn't. Anyway: way back in their history, the Israelites weren't too keen on the Moabites – in fact, they hated the very shadows they cast on the ground.

Recently, the renowned archaeologist Phyllis Stine unearthed an article from an ancient periodical. The bloodstains on the fragment and the way it tails off in mid-sentence suggest that it never saw publication, but Stine's expert team have reconstructed it so that the truth can now be told.

READING BIT

EXCLUSIVE! DARK SECRET AT PALACE

Today, *The Big Round Yellow Thing in the Sky*, the newspaper that brings you the truth first, breaks a scandal that is set to rock the royal palace. Palace authorities are even now desperately seeking ways to trace our courageous undercover reporter (who clearly must remain anonymous) and locate our secret offices so that they can prevent our publishing this story.

We can reveal that King David is the descendant of none other than a Moabite. This sensational story is based on the most reliable evidence from sources close to the king himself. Now, regardless of our own safety, *The Big Round Yellow Thing in the Sky* tells the whole, sordid story.

It began back in the days of the judges, with an Israelite widow called Naomi who emigrated to Moab with her husband and her two sons, who – against all the rules of common decency – married Moabite women. It seems that the men all died in some mysterious way soon afterwards and Naomi was left destitute. So she returned home to Bethlehem, telling her two daughters-in-law, Ruth and Orpah, to stay in Moab and marry Moabite men. Orpah took her advice, but – crucially – Ruth did not. Which fits in with what we know of the Moabite character – stubborn, opinionated and arrogant.

To give her credit, though, from the evidence we have, Ruth does seem to have been a good sort – as Moabites go – and apparently she said something to Naomi about going wherever she went, and dying wherever she died, which really pulls at the old heartstrings, doesn't it? But it doesn't alter the essential fact: she was a Moabite.

The two women came back to Bethlehem, and the plot began to thicken. They needed to earn money of course and, since it was harvest time, Ruth went to work as a gleaner for a farmer called Boaz. Nothing wrong with that – Moabites might be sub-human scum, but we don't mind them doing our dirty work for us, naturally. But the tale doesn't end there. To be fair, we can't blame the Moabite entirely – it seems she was egged on by Naomi, who really should have known better.

Boaz was a single man, with a strong sense of honour, and as it happened he was related to Naomi – and therefore of course to Ruth. He did what any decent man would have done, and gave Ruth protection. We have discovered evidence of special orders given by Boaz to his reapers not to molest Ruth. I bet they loved him for that – everyone knows people like Moabites are fair game. And he showed her kindness, like giving her extra food to take home to Naomi, who of course saw her chance and encouraged a relationship to develop.

Night

A story passed down through a series of reliable sources tells how, one night, Naomi urged Ruth to go and lie down at Boaz's feet. Now, we recognise that Ruth, although a Moabite, was a well-meaning woman – honourable, as far as any Moabite can be. We would not wish to be unjust in portraying this Ruth in an unfair light. No, *The Big Round Yellow Thing in the Sky* is crystal clear: the responsibility lies with Naomi for encouraging her. Clearly, being of a superior race, she should have known better. But be that as it may, the fact remains that these events took place.

Boaz, of course, on waking up and finding her at his feet, could hardly ignore her, which was exactly what Naomi had had in mind. Boaz, again, behaved quite blamelessly. As a relation of Naomi's he had his responsibility, and he had to discharge it.

Next of kin
Here, the story takes another twist. It appears that, although related, Boaz was not the next of kin. There was another (despite extensive enquiries, *The Big Round Yellow Thing in the Sky* has been unable to identify him) who had to be given the chance to honour his obligations, but he wasn't interested. No doubt he knew the kind of problems that a mixed marriage would cause, so he gladly handed over his responsibility to Boaz who, being the innocent he obviously was, married the Moabite and made her respectable.

Line
Now, you may think this is all quite harmless in itself, but *The Big Round Yellow Thing in the Sky* has been able to trace the subsequent events which are devastating.

We have incontrovertible evidence about the line of descent, clearly linking this Moabite woman with King David. Boaz and Ruth had a son called Obed. Obed had a son called Jesse, who took over the family farm in Bethlehem; as we all know, his youngest son, a mere shepherd boy, eventually inveigled his way into the popular affections and now reigns as our king.

The implications of this story are horrendous, flying in the face, as it clearly does, of the stated intention of our forefathers that no Moabite, even until the tenth generation, shall be admitted to the assembly of the Lord.

The *Big Round Yellow Thing in the Sky* says the people are entitled to know the truth. Remember, you heard it first in *The Big Round Yellow Thing . . .*

PRAYING BIT

I've got friends who've had fun made of them
    because of the colour of their hair.
They were bullied for that.
I mean, how stupid can you get?

Obviously very stupid.

We humans are so quick to judge
    and even quicker to lash out
    at what we don't understand
    or don't want to understand.

We use a big word to hide behind:
    prejudice.
At least by using that
    we can pretend someone somewhere
    is doing something about it.

But what we should be bothered about,
    and I mean really bothered,
    is what *we're* doing about it,
    and how we're making a difference.

Because at the moment, Lord,
    we're not.
So help me to be one of the few.

Amen.

Size Isn't Everything

Based on 1 Samuel 17

THINKING BIT

Actually, if you want my opinion, I think the principal difference between David and Goliath is that unlike David, Goliath had a body to match his ego. Just because someone's an underdog doesn't mean they haven't got an outsize opinion of themselves; and be warned: there have been lots of people since David who also thought that God was on their side and that they were infallible, invincible and indispensable – the graveyards are full of them, and only their errors live on.

So don't draw simplistic conclusions from the story, but just reflect that size isn't everything.

READING BIT

'Right, you lily-livered offspring of under-developed small rodents – who's got the guts to fight Goliath?'

Well, no, that probably isn't what Goliath actually said, but since his secretary's dictaphone tape didn't survive, no one knows the exact words. So this is probably near enough – although a good deal more polite, I don't doubt.

Goliath's challenge echoed across the valley separating the Israelite and Philistine armies. The only sound that came back was the sound of the knocking of Israelite knees – not that they were cowards, but when the guy's nine feet tall and uses a rugby post for a baseball bat, anyone with any sense is going to be at least a trifle intimidated.

'I'll cut that arrogant bully down to size!'

The sound of knocking knees was replaced with sharp intakes of Israelite breath, and roars of laughter. David the shepherd boy was your archetypal seven-stone weakling – the kind of chap who doesn't get sand kicked in his face on the beach because even bullies have some standards.

'I'll fight him. I'm not afraid of him – I've frightened wolves away – I've fought lions with my bare hands – I've strangled a bear with one hand while writing my latest hit song with the other – I'm not afraid of anything!'

By this time, most of the soldiers were hoping he would go and fight, because they reckoned Goliath might be able to shut him up. So they took him to the king.

King Saul didn't laugh at David – he just patronised him.

'Now look, son,' he said, 'I know you're probably terrific when it comes to throwing stones at wolves, but this is man's work. When you're a really big boy, perhaps after you've started shaving, you can pop along to the recruiting office and we'll tell you all about a career in the army.'

David hit the roof. 'I keep telling you, God's on my side,' he insisted. 'I'm not afraid of that great big pile of smelly compost out there,' – which only goes to show that some of the people on God's 'side' can be just as polite, or not, as anyone else when it suits them. Anyway, Saul eventually gave in.

'Okay, okay, don't lose your rag – it's all you're wearing. If you insist, you can go and fight, but you'll need some armour.' So they got Saul's spare helmet and breastplate, and put them on David.

'Hey! who turned the light out? And get this wagon off me, so I can stand up again.'

Well, you can send a boy to fight a man's battles, but apparently not in a man's armour. So David went out to face Goliath wearing his bit of old sack and carrying his security blanket – a strip of goatskin he'd taken to using for throwing stones. On the way, he stopped at the stream for ammunition – some nice, smooth stones that wouldn't jam in the sling. Then he strode off with all the confidence of inexperience, up the hillside toward Goliath.

'What's this?' Goliath was insulted – and who can blame him. His therapist had told him all about reverse psychology, and he recognised a hidden statement when he saw it. 'Are you trying to take the . . . '

'Shut it, and listen, you great gob of warm lager!' David wasn't to be out-done – it's not the size of the mouth that counts, but what comes out of it. 'I've got God on my side – and he's going to help me kick your shins.'

I don't suppose God was particularly proud of that kind of talk, but then God isn't into pride – and it wasn't the first time, nor would it be the last, that he'd been embarrassed by people who said they were working for him.

Goliath let out an almighty roar, picked up his rugby post and prepared to hurl it at David – not a nice prospect, to put it mildly. David wasn't afraid, though – he hadn't learnt about fear, yet, because he'd never been to a church council meeting. He just fished a stone out of his bag and put it into the sling. Goliath couldn't believe what he was seeing. With an army equipped with all the latest weaponry, they were sending out a boy to throw stones at him. That was the crucial moment. Goliath blinked in astonishment and never even saw the stone that killed him.

Thwack! It landed right in the middle of his forehead, with enough force to kill his brain cell before it had even had time to find a mate and breed. Goliath's rugby post hit the deck just before he did (even dropping dead was a ponderous business for Goliath) and David went and unsheathed the giant's sword.

That's the trouble with children – they never know when to stop. Not content with having killed and humiliated the guy, he cut off Goliath's head and waved it at the crowd who immediately went wild and made David a national hero – amazing, when you think he'd never played football.

That night they sat around the campfire, and David sang a song he'd written all by himself:

God loves the humble people,
and puts the proud to shay-ay-ay-ayme!

That's the wonderful thing about God. He uses the most amazing people!

PRAYING BIT

David.
What's all that about then?
You, Lord, once again,
    chose the least obvious
    to beat the opposition.
Brilliant and daring in one punch.

Now, Lord,
    I'm not saying I've got aspirations to be king
    or go out killing giants,
    but I wouldn't mind thinking that perhaps
    this seven-stone weakling
    could be used in a similar way.

I want my life to be surprising,
    to be different.
There are plenty of giants to be knocked down today anyway,
    and although they're not big hairy blokes
    with big swords
    they're frightening enough.

I know I can't battle single-handed
    against poverty, homelessness, hunger . . .
But perhaps with a few stones
    I can make a dent or two,
    knock them off balance?

Be my sling, Lord.

Amen.

Consequences

Based on 2 Samuel 11

THINKING BIT

'I can resist anything except temptation,' wrote Oscar Wilde, which rather suggests that exposing oneself to it is a touch risky. Now, of course, all of life's a risk, and we can't avoid that, but you don't go white-water rafting on an inflatable bed if all you've got the skill for is a paddle-boat on the pond in a leisure park.

But then, there's always someone who will – and I suppose you have to have just that kind of mentality to claw your way up the political tree the way David did.

READING BIT

I'm not sure when it was that king David found out that his palace overlooked his neighbour's bathroom. I wouldn't entirely put it past him to have arranged things that way – he was a cunning old character, was David – but that's just my idle speculation so don't let it go any further. Right? And I don't know how much time he'd spent idly walking about on the flat roof of his house, before he got 'lucky' – but let's get to the point.

There he was, walking on the roof, the way you do, when he just happened to glance in through the bathroom window of the said neighbour, Bathsheba, just as she was in the tub, the altogether, and no state to receive visitors. Well, she was a very beautiful woman and David was a very ordinary man in that respect, so the temptation to keep looking was hard to resist – and he decided not to. If he'd known where it might lead, he just might have settled for a blind eye, a cold shower and a solitary mug of cocoa, but by the time he thought of that he wasn't thinking straight.

'It doesn't actually hurt to look, does it!' he thought to himself. 'If she wanted privacy she should have drawn the blind. I bet she wanted me to see her – that's it – it's all her fault.' And that provided David with all the justification he felt he needed to keep on looking.

'I mean, it's not my fault she just happens to be in my line of sight, is it?' he thought again, as he leaned perilously over the parapet and craned his neck round the corner of the east wing of the palace for a better view.

Well, one thing generally leads to another in cases like this, and David, of course, was a very powerful man – which made him all the more vulnerable where temptation is concerned. He was the king. He could have whatever he wanted. And since the king was God's representative to the people, well, he was almost like God, wasn't he – so he really ought to be above the law, and anyway it wouldn't do any harm. Bathsheba's husband was away at the war, so she must be lonely. Of course! That was why she'd flaunted herself at him in that way, he thought, almost falling over the rail in his attempt to keep her in view when she got out of the bath.

By now, he'd just about convinced himself that whatever he wanted was okay – which was a pity, because it wasn't. And in particular, what he wanted at that moment very definitely wasn't okay.

So it wasn't long before she was round at the palace, savouring the delights of the royal cuisine and beginning to think similar thoughts to David's. Now, you might say it takes two to tango, but when one party is an absolute monarch and the other is a vulnerable subject with no rights or security and is thought of as property – not that that absolved of her responsibility – well, it makes the whole thing a bit uneven, wouldn't you say? So it didn't take too long before her visits to David took too long, and I imagine you can conceive of the eventual outcome.

'What do you mean, "pregnant"?', David roared. 'How did that happen?'

Bathsheba decided that King David was just a little too old for the 'birds and the bees' bit, and satisfied herself with giving him an old-fashioned look (which is all they should have given each other in the first place, of course).

'It's alright for you,' she said, 'but what am I going to do when Uriah throws me out? Since he's been away killing, pillaging and generally doing your dirty work for the last six months, I somehow don't think we'll be able to fool him that it's his, do you?'

It was a bit late to make a mental note never to look into women's bathrooms again: David had to find a way out. He didn't like the idea of murder – it's not the sort of thing any of us does lightly, is it? I mean, I don't suppose any of us has ever put out a contract on somebody without, at least, a little pang of guilt?

But David decided it was necessary under the circumstances. After all, it would be terribly bad for the national interest if he got found out, wouldn't it? This just wasn't the right time for a change of government – especially as changes of government tended to be quite bloody affairs at that time – and he dreaded to think of the effect on foreign confidence in the shekel. It took him no time at all to convince himself that he was doing it for the sake of the nation. He sent a message to the commander of his army.

Bathsheba's husband Uriah thought it was a great honour being asked to lead the next charge: the king must have real confidence in his ability. He'd always known, he thought with pride, that one day King David would realise he had something special – which of course was just what King David had realised: and he wanted her.

Uriah never saw the sword that killed him – and he never got to enjoy his hero status, either. It was a truly impressive funeral: everyone shed tears for him, and David said what a wonderful, brave soldier he was. The whole nation took him to their hearts – and David took his widow to his bed. Well, she was upset; he felt he ought to comfort her.

Of course, David knew it hadn't been right – but that's life, isn't it, full of difficult choices. Perhaps with hindsight he should have pulled himself up short before things got out of hand, but how could he be expected to foresee the consequences? Anyway, it was alright now – he'd be good from now on – and since no one knew the truth it would all be okay.

But Someone did know . . .

PRAYING BIT

You do pick them, Lord.
David was great
    and David wasn't.
Misused his power,
    messed everything up . . .
    and you chose him.

I don't suppose you ever regretted that, did you?
I guess not.
You pretty much know what you're doing
    and seem able to make good
    out of a really lousy situation.

David was brilliant
    and bad.
He was a great leader
    and a weak man.
But you used him,
    despite of,
    and because of,
    his weaknesses.

Which makes David so much more approachable.
He's not perfect,
    he's not a shiny, haloed, glowing individual.
He's got more baggage than a bus load
    of retired tourists visiting Bournemouth.
He does good and bad.
And does both really rather well.

And if you can use someone like that
    you can use me.
Please?

Amen.

What a Nerve!

Based on 2 Samuel 12

THINKING BIT

Getting angry about injustice is the easy part. Actually getting the powers that be to listen and do something about it is quite another matter. You need to box clever.

READING BIT

Nathan the prophet was enjoying a well-earned rest. 'That's the good thing about this king,' he said to his neighbour, 'He's a good one – cares about justice, thinks the ordinary people matter, that kind of thing. Makes life much easier for me, I don't mind telling you – not to say, safer.'

'I dunno,' his neighbour replied. 'I'm not much into politics, myself, but at the end of the day they're all the same, you know.'

'Not this one,' Nathan insisted. 'I'm happy with this one.'

Before his neighbour could say anything else, God did.

'I think you and I need a quiet word, Nathan,' he said. 'Let's go somewhere private so your neighbour doesn't think you've lost it when you start talking to thin air, and have you whisked away and diagnosed with something long-winded.'

Once safely out of earshot of others, God continued, 'It's King David. He's gone and blotted his copy-book – and I mean big time. Your job is to go and tell him the error of his ways.'

That didn't sound very healthy to Nathan. He might have thought David was a good king, but that's when you measure him against other kings, not by normal standards of decency. And anyway, if, as it appeared, David was getting too big for his boots, then all bets were off as far as Nathan was concerned. Still, when you're a Hebrew prophet, that's how the bagel crumbles and you just have to live with it.

'Okay, okay,' he said. 'What's he done now – made one of his slaves work overtime, or forgotten a ritual sacrifice?'

'Adultery,' came the reply, 'with Uriah the Hittite's wife – followed by murder and blatant hypocrisy in public worship.'

'Go on!' exclaimed Nathan, incredulously. So God did.

'He had an affair with Bathsheba, and then when she got pregnant he had her husband killed.'

Suddenly, Nathan didn't feel afraid any more – just angry.

'I'll sort him out – trust me!' he growled.

'Well, play it canny,' God remonstrated. 'The point is to make him see he's done wrong, not just go and pick a fight to make yourself feel better.'

David was surprised to see Nathan, and thought it must be a festival he'd forgotten about. 'I'm sorry, Nathan – affairs of state you know.'

'A state of affairs, more like,' Nathan muttered, careful not to let David hear him, but then more loudly: 'Actually, Your Majesty, I've come to see you about another matter – a question of justice.'

David was interested straight away. He prided himself on standing up for justice, which just goes to show how selective some people's consciences can be. 'Go on, Nathan.'

'Thank you, Your Majesty. It's come to my attention that a grave injustice has been perpetrated by a powerful man against someone much weaker.' Seeing David's attentive expression, he went on: 'A poor man had a pet lamb – not very much to anyone else, but it was his only friend in the world, as well as his sole possession. You just can't imagine how much he loved that lamb.'

David was getting even more interested at that point – it sounded like a wonderful scenario for a songwriter trying to break into the secular market. He was already humming a tune to himself when he realised Nathan was still talking.

'Well, there's this neighbour, see – rich guy, pots of money, flocks of sheep all over the place – and as tight as a chancellor's fist. Anyway, this neighbour had a friend visiting him and wanted to give him a good meal. So what does he do – kill one of his own sheep? Not on your life, he doesn't – just takes this poor man's little pet lamb and has it on the menu before you can say, "Gross injustice and misuse of executive power".'

'I'll kill him!' roared David. 'That'll teach him a lesson he's not likely to forget, won't it! By the time I've finished with him he'll know better than to exploit poor, vulnerable people – and lambs. Tell me who he is – come on, now, no shilly-shallying just because he's got a few shekels. Who is he?'

'You.'

'Right! Off with his head! Stick it on a pole on the city wall! I want everyone to know that I don't stand for any grotesque barbarity. I'll make an example of . . . Who did you say it was?'

'You, Your Majesty. You've got a harem full of wives here, but it wasn't enough for you, was it? Oh, no. Uriah had just one wife and he loved her to distraction. So you had him killed so you could take her, and now you've added her to your selection box. Now, what was it you were saying about barbarity?'

You've got to give David his due: he didn't try and wheedle out of it. 'I've done wrong,' he said, 'and I deserve to be punished.'

Well, to cut a long story short, the baby David and Bathsheba were expecting, died. They all thought it was God's punishment. To be quite candid, I'd take some convincing that God would kill a baby to punish its parents, and if you did manage to convince me I'd lose the inclination to worship a god like that. But as metaphors go it does make the point rather well: children in that culture represented the future, and a future that's worth having can't be built on injustice.

PRAYING BIT

Well, Lord,
    when I say I'd like to be like David,
    I don't mean literally.
So you probably won't need
    a Nathan to come and tell me how bad I've been . . .
    I hope.

I know I do bad things,
    like anyone.
Some I mean to do,
    others I don't.
And sometimes I secretly think,
    'It's OK, God will forgive me.'
Which isn't very clever, is it?
(At least I've admitted it.)

I know you forgive,
    but that's not an excuse
    to do what I want,
    when I want,
    and then try to cover it up.
Or pretend it's OK
    because no one else knows.

But I do use it as an excuse,
    and I'm sorry.
I don't mean to be weak,
    but I am.

Build me, Lord,
    make me strong.

Amen.

Love You To Bits

Based on 1 Kings 3:16-27

THINKING BIT

Okay, so threatening to cut someone's baby in half isn't a particularly great sign of wisdom – but there was some pretty shrewd psychology behind it. And the sight of parents, centuries later, treating children like possessions must make us wonder whether his insight into the nature of love was a bit more advanced than ours is sometimes.

READING BIT

'You get your thieving little paws out of my underwear drawer!'

'I'm only taking what's mine – why can't you buy your own?'

'I wouldn't be seen dead in anything of yours – and talking of death, if those aren't back in my drawer in ten seconds . . .'

The neighbours were used to this kind of thing, and knew what to expect. Sure enough, the sound of ripping fabric soon tore its way through the thin walls.

'Now look what you've done!'

'I don't care – at least you can't wear it any more!'

That's how life always was for Lizzie and Rachel. Back in the days of King Solomon there weren't many employment opportunities for women (he might have been wise but he wasn't that wised up) and they made their living the only way they knew how. They shared a flat out of sheer economic necessity, and certainly not because they had any great affection for each other, so rows of this kind were an everyday event – as were torn clothes, victims of their tug-of-war quarrels.

'One day,' a neighbour commented, 'it won't be clothes they're tearing apart. It's the kids I feel sorry for.'

To be fair, Rachel and Lizzie were good mums insofar as they were able to be – but they just couldn't help letting the rivalry show even in that aspect of their lives. They both spent all the time they could with their new babies, and they even began to co-operate by child-minding for each other. For a while it seemed as though the babies might bring them together, but that hope came to an abrupt and ghastly end.

One night, Lizzie got up in the early hours and went to check on her baby. The cot seemed strangely still – no little snuffles and snores, and the bedclothes not moving in their usual rhythmic way. Lizzie touched Ben's cheek. He was cold. Stone cold.

Lizzie was desperate – and to give her her due, she was hardly in a state to think clearly as, with tears of grief and rage streaming down her face, she tip-toed over to Rachel's bedside where Joel was fast asleep in his cot. The babies were uncannily alike, otherwise Lizzie would never have dared to do what she did, even in the state she was in. Very gently, so as not to risk making him cry and waking Rachel, she lifted Joel out of his cot and put Ben where he had been. She knew then that she'd got to put on a very brave act indeed – so somehow she stopped the tears and applied a quick bit of make-up to disguise her red, swollen eyes. Then she tip-toed back to her own bed, leaving Rachel's baby Joel in her dead baby's cot.

The rest of the night was horrible. She hated herself for what she'd done – even though they quarrelled like cat and dog she would never have wanted Rachel's baby to die, and while she'd always known herself to be no angel she wouldn't have expected herself to behave like that. But she was desperate for a baby – Ben had been the only good thing in her life, and in a strange way he'd made her feel human for the first time. Not that she felt particularly human at that moment, mind you, but she hoped the guilt would pass. All this and much more went through her mind as she lay there, choking back tears and dreading the moment when Rachel would wake up.

Of course, when Rachel did wake up, it got worse. For some strange reason she couldn't fully understand, Lizzie wanted to go and comfort her but of course that was impossible. It wasn't long before the screams, accusations and counter-accusations seared through the walls and the horrified neighbours decided the time had come for action. 'There's only one person who can settle this,' grumbled one sleepy-eyed woman. 'You're going to the king, whether you like it or not.'

So it was that, before he'd even had time to take the rollers out of his beard, King Solomon was confronted by two ferocious women and an exasperated group of neighbours. Well, he tried everything. He compared the shapes of noses, the colour of hair, the wideness of the eyes, but he had to admit that the babies were much too alike, and much too unlike their mothers, for him to be able to get a clue. He was a compassionate man, though, and he desperately wanted to make sure that the right mother got the living baby. He was sorry for whoever had lost hers, of course, but that wouldn't be helped by stealing someone else's.

Suddenly he had a brainwave. 'I wonder which one of these women loves the live baby the most,' he thought. Careful not to give the game away, he put on his solemn face and said, 'I've decided that as we can't tell whose the baby is, you can have half each. That's fair, isn't it?'

At first, no one believed him, but he put little Joel on the table and raised his sword high. 'Half each,' he repeated. 'Okay?'

Lizzie was horrified – stealing Rachel's baby was bad enough, but to have him killed as well . . . Still, she could hardly own up, so she just gritted her teeth and said, 'Sounds fair enough to me.'

Rachel couldn't believe it at first – was the king really going to do this? In the nick of time, she found her voice: 'No! No! No! If I've got to lose him, I've got to lose him – but please don't harm him. Give him to her. Please give him to her.'

Solomon breathed a huge sigh of relief as he put down the sword, gently picked Joel up and passed him to Rachel. 'Here you are,' he said. 'Take your baby.'

From that day on, Lizzie and Rachel never quarrelled again – but only because they never spoke again. Any hope they might ever have had of learning to be friends had gone. Like it or not, they had to stop sharing the flat, and Lizzie, for the first time in her life, did the decent thing. She moved out. She would never be able to forgive herself for what she'd done, or get over the loss of her baby. Nonetheless, in a strange sort of way, she felt relieved.

PRAYING BIT

Solomon.
Wise?
Mad?
Both?
Mr Extreme Measures, methinks.
Don't think I'd be of the 'cutting a baby in half' brigade,
    but I see why he suggested it.

I'm trying to work out what this is telling me.
After all,
    people are always saying I should read the Bible,
    understand from it,
    learn from it.
Well, I'm not.
Not in this case, anyway.
What's swords and babies got to do
    with me and where I am?
Seems very strange
    and irrelevant.

Sorry if that's rude,
    but it's how I feel.
And if I'm to learn
    I've got to say when I'm not.

Help me understand, Lord,
    and give me patience when I don't.

Amen.

Elemental, My Dear Elijah

Based on 1 Kings 19:1-18

THINKING BIT

Okay, so Elijah wasn't the first person – and he certainly wouldn't be the last – to think that he was the only true friend God had. More to the point, Queen Jezebel wasn't the first and certainly wouldn't be the last powerful ruler to get hysterical about prophets who 'mix religion and politics'. How often are we going to have to repeat the elementary point that if God cares about the powerless, he presumably cares about the *causes* of their powerlessness – political, economic, or whatever?

READING BIT

'I don't care if he's the Great High Priest of Wannamakalulu – he's dead meat. I want him brought back here alive so that I can disembowel him with my own fingernails. Understand?'

Queen Jezebel was having a good day – by her standards. She'd started off by having the chamber maid beheaded for forgetting to put out a clean hand towel, and that had given her an appetite for what she called 'defending the National Interest' which somehow or other always seemed to coincide with her interests and invariably involved the palace staff in overtime scrubbing blood off the walls.

But now she'd discovered the greatest threat yet to the National Interest – some jumped-up religious type was getting political, and if there's one thing tyrannical dictators hate it's people who mix politics with religion. And Elijah had committed the cardinal sin of all political clerics – he'd been shown to be right. So of course he had to go.

Elijah went. Very quickly indeed. As soon as he got word that the Jazzy Belle was after him, he just took to his heels and legged it to the desert where he sat down to recover his breath and his self-pity.

'No one understands me,' he moaned. 'No one cares about

the truth except me. Everyone's wrong and only I'm right. I wish I was dead!'

Now, you've got to give God credit – he tried. He gave Elijah a nice sleep and baked him a cake ready for when he woke up – even being thoughtful enough to provide some water to wash it down with. Now, I ask you – what more could Elijah ask for? You'd have thought a tough dude like Elijah could have found the courage to face up to a painted lady with a vicious temper, a large army and absolute power, wouldn't you? Well, he couldn't. He just got up again and traipsed off further into the desert until he came to a cave.

By this time it was obvious to God that little titbits like hot cakes and water weren't going to be effective. Elijah wasn't in any condition to take hints, so a more direct approach was required.

'Hey! Elijah! What are you doing here?'

'Oh, God!' Elijah moaned. 'Everyone's against me. They've killed all your prophets, torn down your temples and smashed up the altars . . . I'm the only friend you've got left in the whole wide world – and they're after me, as well, now.'

'Oh, my life, not another one!' thought God. 'I suppose I'd better let him down gently – let him think that he's worked it out all by himself.' Then he said, 'Go outside, Elijah – no, don't argue – for once, just do as I ask without trying to get your brain cell round it. Right. About time, too. Now, whatever happens, you stay out here and don't go skulking back into the cave. Okay?'

Before Elijah had time to answer, a Tornado lashed into the side of the mountain – which surprised Elijah because he'd never even heard of the Wright brothers, let alone the RAF.

'Oops, sorry – wrong millennium,' said God. 'Hey, Gabriel – change that capital 'T' to a lower case and fax it again. We'll have to speak to the agency about that temp.'

This time, it was right – a tornado of amazing force pinned Elijah against the mountainside. Elijah was impressed – but try as he might he couldn't find God in the wind at all.

Next came the earthquake – like the Glastonbury Festival without the restraint – but God wasn't in that, either (and who can blame him, you might ask). Elijah was almost past caring by now, anyway – after all, even a charismatic prophet doesn't like things too manic.

Just as things seemed to be getting calmer, the whole place erupted in flames: huge, monstrous, vicious beasties, threatening to devour everything in their path – particularly frightening for someone of Elijah's sheltered upbringing who'd never been to a Parliamentary debate in his life. It about did it for Elijah – he'd had all the drama he could handle this side of a cherry brandy. Then he heard a sound – a tiny, murmuring voice that asked, 'Tell me again, Elijah: what are you doing here?'

'Oh, well that's easy – it's because of my great love for you, Lord, my zeal for the truth, my commitment to evangelism and social action. I'm the only one who understands that you need both in this modern world – all the others are dead, and your temples are destroyed, and I'm the only one left who's got it right.'

'Yeah, yeah, so you've said. Elijah, get off your rump and go and look and you'll find there are a few more out there – like 7000. There's a new king to anoint (not to mention a new prophet for you to train to take your place) – just because they haven't been making as much noise as you have doesn't mean they aren't there. I don't always work through the stirrers and the shakers, you know.'

So Elijah went.

So did Queen Jezebel – but much more painfully. Which just goes to show that noise and authority are not quite the same thing.

Try telling that to your MP at election time.

PRAYING BIT

Lord,
    loads of Christians seem to be really obvious about it.
They talk about it,
    know the Bible back to front,
    have a prayer for everything,
    love you,
    tell everyone about the above four,
    and apparently don't sleep
    because they're too busy praying.

I'm not . . .
    obvious, that is, about being a Christian.
At least I don't think so.
I'm fairly scared of talking about it,
    I don't read the Bible much,
    I pray about a few things occasionally,
    and I think I love you.
What does that mean?
What does it say about me?
What does it say about them?
What does it say about you?
What am I on about?

But I believe in you, which is a start.
And I do pray.
And some other stuff.
Is that OK for starters?
If so, can we make the main course
    really really appetising?

Cheers, Lord.

Amen.

I'm Not Prejudiced, But . . .

Based on the Book of Jonah

THINKING BIT

'I'm not prejudiced, but . . .'

The most deadly kind of prejudice is the subtle kind that begins by convincing its owner that it doesn't exist. It masquerades as loyalty, or patriotism, or commitment to one's own ('Charity begins at home') – and other qualities we can allow ourselves to think of as virtuous. And then it's deadly, because it's impossible to convince wonderful, lovely, respectable people who cherish their families, pay their taxes and give generously to charity that they're nursing a viper in their bosom.

Even God has sometimes had to resort to some pretty desperate tactics.

READING BIT

To watch Jonah play with his children, you wouldn't have thought the word 'hate' was even in his vocabulary. In fact, there were just two things Jonah hated: prejudice and foreigners. Of course, he didn't actually realise that he hated foreigners: it seemed reasonable to him that people who were different should keep away from each other and not interfere in each other's lives. 'Live and let live' was his motto – and preferably at a distance. That wasn't prejudice – just realism. If God had meant people to mix he wouldn't have made them so different.

And as for those people who insisted on interfering in the affairs of other nations – he thought they'd really got a nerve. 'People should be free to make their own choices,' he said to his children, 'and we should leave them to learn from their mistakes.'

So saying, and ignoring her howls of protest, he picked up his baby daughter, just in time to stop her freely choosing to play with the pretty, bright-red logs on the fire.

That night, as he said his prayers, he asked, as usual, 'Lord, what would you really like me to do for you?' As usual, he got no reply and dozed off, happy that he'd shown God how willing he was. But he didn't sleep well that night – for some strange reason he just couldn't get Nineveh out of his mind. Nineveh was one of those foreign places where people did really unpleasant things to each other, and everyone knew it couldn't go on – the whole society was disintegrating around them. Jonah couldn't understand why it was on his mind. One thing he was sure of (well, almost sure – well, fairly sure . . .) was that God wouldn't send him there! So why did he keep on thinking about it?

As time went on he came to regret all those prayers when he'd asked God to tell him what to do. Why couldn't he have just kept his big mouth shut! (Himself, he meant, not God . . . or did he?)

'Look,' he said one night, 'I'm not prejudiced, but charity begins at home.'

'Maybe, maybe not,' God replied, 'but why does it have to end there? You've done a good job at home, and I think you'd benefit from a broader perspective on life.'

Well, if what God wanted him to do was broaden his perspective, he could go somewhere nice. Spain would be good – full of foreigners, of course, but they're okay when you're a tourist and they have to treat you with respect. So Spain it was. He kissed his wife and children goodbye (after all, God wanted him to broaden his mind, and he could hardly do that and child-mind at the same time, could he?) and went and got on the boat. Nothing like a good sea voyage to broaden the mind. And it certainly broadened Jonah's.

Just as he'd got comfy in his deck-chair, he heard a shout from the crow's nest: 'Fasten everything down – there's a storm on the horizon.' He didn't take much notice, though – what do crows know about weather? So he just stayed in his chair and dozed off. What a nightmare! He dreamt he was on a roller-coaster at a Spanish seaside resort. Now there were just two things that worried him: foreign safety standards, and the fact that roller coasters weren't due to be invented for about 3000 years. The latter point seemed a touch academic as the manic machine hurtled up and down, rolling from side to side and threatening to show the entire world that his breakfast hadn't been kosher. Then the rain hit him and he woke up.

He and his deckchair were sliding separately around the deck of the boat as it pitched and tossed on the sea. Grabbing hold of the rail as he collided with it, he dragged himself upright and back to his senses.

'It's all my fault,' he thought. 'I'd better do as God told me.' So he struggled over to where the Captain was trying to control the ship.

'Don't just stand there,' yelled the captain. 'Pray. We've got distress calls going out to every conceivable deity, and nothing's happening – perhaps yours can help.'

'Oh, he can,' said Jonah. 'Just throw me overboard.'

Sounds a bit extreme, but Jonah had it all worked out. As soon as he hit the water, God would pull him out again and magically set him on the shore of Nineveh. After all, that was what God wanted, so he'd be a bit daft to let him drown. So to Jonah it was all quite cut-and-dried, but not to the captain who had never in 30 years at sea thrown a paying passenger overboard.

'Oh, don't worry,' Jonah assured him loftily. 'My God's better than all your other rotten gods put together. My God will save me because I'm important to him.'

The captain decided to throw Jonah overboard.

God didn't quite work to Jonah's schedule, though. Oh, he picked him up alright, and took him to Nineveh, but it was a bit less simple than that. As soon as the big fish opened its mouth and swallowed him, Jonah just knew it was going to get complicated – you know how you sometimes just get that feeling? So there he sat, in a stomach the size of a rock singer's mouth, wondering what to do next.

He knew he'd have to get out one way or the other, and either way would be unpleasant (and totally unacceptable to the readers of religious books). So he prayed. There's something about being surrounded by half-digested fish and rotting seaweed that concentrates the mind, and Jonah suddenly knew what God was saying to him.

Three days later, smelly but chastened, Jonah was vomited up ('Praise be to God for choosing the lesser of the two evils') on the shore of Nineveh. He preached, they repented, and he learned a valuable lesson.

'If ever I go to sea again,' he said, 'I'm going to wear a T-shirt with "Trust the Tabloid Press" written on it. There's not a fish in the world would swallow that.'

PRAYING BIT

I'm not, Lord,
    prejudiced, that is.
At least I didn't think so;
    until today.

This kid in class,
    the weird skinny one with spots and smells
    (as in aromas that make your stomach churn)
    was being annoying.
Well, he was sat at the front
    asking questions
    and answering, too.
Just how spoddy is that?

So after lessons
    some of the class made fun of him,
    threw his bag on the roof
    and we all laughed.

Not clever . . . or nice.
Just stupid
    and prejudiced
    against someone who was 'different'.
That's it.
And I'm sorry.

Because it's made me realise
    that if it can happen in school
    to someone with spots
    who knows the answers,
    what if it happens
    in a country
    to thousands who believe
    or look different?

We're a stained society, Lord.
Wash us.

Amen.

Only Following Orders

Based on Matthew 2:16-18

THINKING BIT

What makes ordinary human beings do horribly inhuman things? Are those who give the orders and those who carry them out completely different, or are there similarities in the pressures to which they respond? I don't suppose any of us is ever going to kill a townful of infants, but are there other, lesser ways in which we, too, find ourselves under pressure and respond in ways that surprise us?

As this is being written, Albanians are being 'ethnically cleansed' in Kosovo, and not just governments but ordinary people are doing things of which they would never have thought themselves capable. By the time you read this, pray God, the Kosovo crisis will be over, but it will be happening somewhere, whether in Africa or, on a smaller scale, on a British housing estate.

What kind of fear so dehumanises those whom God has made in his image?

READING BIT

Look, I'm not a politician. I'm a soldier. I don't know the ins and outs of government decisions – I'm just paid to implement them. And the order was simple: kill all the boy babies in Bethlehem under the age of two. No one liked it, of course, but we weren't in any position to argue. Now, if you'd asked me, in a purely hypothetical way, would I ever kill a baby, I'd probably have punched you in the mouth. Me? Violent? Never! But this was duty, and I didn't have any choice.

As far as I can make out, King Herod had had a visit from some soothsayer characters – Eastern astrologers, apparently – who were looking for a new-born king. Now if he'd asked my advice, I'd have told him to ignore them; these are modern times and we don't go for all that supernatural stuff – but Herod just couldn't get it out of his head that what they'd said fitted in with some ancient prophecy or other. Well, you know and I know that almost anything can be interpreted as fulfilling a prophecy if you're determined enough, but he wasn't having any of that. Before we knew it, he'd got it firmly into his head that there was a baby boy, somewhere in Bethlehem, sucking contentedly at some mother's breast and, even as he did so, entertaining political ambitions. There's no reasoning with that kind of mentality, is there?

After a few days, these wise guys hadn't returned (as they'd agreed to do) to tell Herod where the king was. So the paranoid old wind-break got the idea they'd rumbled him. He'd made out he wanted to go and worship the child, but it was obvious what he really wanted to do – and that they were deliberately avoiding him. Life at the palace was hell, I don't mind telling you. Every time an unexplained shadow moved within 100 metres, the king threw a wobbly and some poor sucker of a guard's head received its independence. By the time the king really lost it, we'd all got thoroughly scared and would have done anything he told us without a second thought. No, not 'would have' – we did.

It was about three-thirty in the morning when we heard blood-curdling screams from the king's sleeping quarters. 'Aaaaaggghhhh! Treason! Treachery!' Obviously, the old fool was having another of his nightmares, but we all knew what that meant by now: another head about to go bouncing down the palace steps with a great big empty space where its neck should be. We all looked apprehensively at one another, with that dreadful feeling: 'I hope it's one of you.' Then I heard a sound that made my blood run cold.

'Guard Commander!' Oh, my life – he was going to the top, in more ways than one. I knew trying to get away would only prolong the agony, so I decided to face the ordeal like a soldier, and went in. But Herod had a surprise for me.

'Stop shaking in your shoes, you miserable coward,' he shrieked hysterically, 'I'm not after your head, so get a grip.' As he said this, his trembling hand reached for the bottle beside his bed and he swigged at it compulsively. 'I can't go on like this, I simply can't go on. I want every baby boy in Bethlehem got rid of. Understand? Each and every boy under 2 years old – kill them! Hunt them down! I won't rest until I know they're all dead.'

I just stood there. Now I knew he'd really got a problem. I was about to ask for the order in writing when he screamed at me again. 'What are you waiting for? Get out and get on, or I'll start with you first!'

That was not the time to point out that I was a touch more than two years old, so I saluted and backed out. No, not as a mark of respect – this was Herod's palace, not the court of Windsor – I just didn't want to take my eyes off the barmy old fool.

I had to get tough with the men, to make them do it. None of them wanted to, but when I pointed out that most of them had wives and children whom Herod might use as substitutes if they refused, they saw the wisdom of obedience soon enough.

So we rode into Bethlehem. At first, no one took much notice – they were used to soldiers passing through – and we were able to position ourselves well before we started. Then I just called out, 'Now!' and all hell broke loose. As the swords came out, people began to panic and to run, and when the first child fell the screams became unbearable. But we had our duty, so we did what we always do in such cases: we went into auto-response mode and just got on with it – coldly, clinically, like any other military operation.

But of course it wasn't. Those screams drove themselves through my brain like nails through a crucified criminal. Except they didn't kill me, that would have been a merciful thing. No, they just stayed there, echoing and re-echoing like a nightmare you can't wake up from. I've prayed to the gods, I've made sacrifices, I've done penances, but to no avail. For 30 years I've prayed to die: I've taken risks no soldier would ever take, but somehow I always seem to survive. I don't mind telling you, I'm at my wits' end. I'm getting so desperate, I'm even turning to the Jewish religion.

They've got this rabbi – must have been born at about the

time of the massacre, I'd say – he seems to have something no one else has, and he says anything can be forgiven. Anything . . . I'm going to go and see him. Yes, I know it sounds crazy, but when you're feeling the way I am you'll grab any straw that's going. Say a prayer for me, won't you.

PRAYING BIT

The trouble with me, Lord,
   (What? There's only one?)
   is that when I read the Bible,
   I don't read it.
I don't look behind the scenes
   to try and imagine what else was going on.

Take the soldiers that carried out the slaughter:
   what happened to them?
Did some of them turn to you?
Now there's a thought;
   someone sent to kill you
   ends up following you –
   kind of a full circle.

And then there are all the other characters:
What about the soldiers who crucified you?
And the people at the wedding with the wine incident?
Or the 5000?

So much was going on
   and we miss it because we're blind to it
   and don't want to look any further.

But maybe,
   just maybe,
   it's by looking that little bit further
   that we start to learn.

Amen.

Untouchable

Based on Matthew 8:1-4

THINKING BIT

I listened in horror to what my companion was saying: 'If it were down to me, I'd gas all the homosexuals and send the blacks back home – that's the only answer to AIDS.' As he spoke, he tenderly cradled his severely mentally disabled daughter whom he loved and cared for with a devotion few of us could even imagine. He was actually a good man. But he was a frightened man with whom, on this point, it proved utterly impossible to reason.

In the mid-eighties, no one knew much about AIDS except that it killed people, horribly – but there were lost of scary ideas about. In addition, it became a way of demonising those minorities of whom some sectors of society were already afraid. The few churches that had the faith and courage to try and help sufferers lost members and risked arson attacks; and the government's poster campaign ('Don't die of ignorance') typically blamed the victim, created fear, and unwittingly revealed where the most frightening ignorance was truly to be found. No society and no generation is immune from fear such as that, or from the distorting effects it has upon good, compassionate human beings.

READING BIT

Joe had everything a young man in first-century Palestine could ask for: good looks, fast camels, the lot. He was never short of company, especially the young, attractive feminine kind, and he had a bright future ahead of him managing – and eventually, it was simply assumed – inheriting his father's farm.

Then it started – gradually at first, but rapidly getting worse: the skin problem. To begin with he didn't take a lot of notice – a few blackheads were to be expected at his age, and he'd grow out of them before long; they'd go away. They didn't: they burst. Then came the boils, springing up like weeds in a warm, wet summer and refusing to go away. By now, Joe had only a vague idea how ghastly he looked because he'd long since given up looking in mirrors – apart from anything else he didn't need to because the people he used to call 'friends' delighted in describing his appearance to him in graphic detail:

'Well, I wouldn't say it was bad, but if I were a dog I wouldn't lick it.'

'Until I knew you I thought lava only came from volcanoes.'

'Why don't you bottle that stuff and sell it as slug bait?'

And they were the printable ones.

Before long, though, people stopped saying nasty things to Joe. In fact thy stopped talking to him altogether: the nearest he got to communication was the stones they threw at him if he got too close. Then the farm business collapsed; no one was going to buy food from a member of his family.

'It's no use,' said his father. 'We'll just have to sell up.'

That proved more easily said than done, though. No one knew what the cause of Joe's condition was, but some rumours sprung up that it was an allergy to something in the soil. Before long there were heated debates in the market place about whether it could get into the food chain and some government officials who knew a lot less than they thought they did, put a ban on all the produce.

Joe's parents had to take a tough decision. 'Sorry, son, but it's you or us. You'll have to go away. Don't worry, though, we'll come and visit you.'

They did, too. They came every day, and the fact that the place Joe was in was full of people as ill as he was, or worse, didn't seem to put them off. But gradually, they were able to bring him less and less because they themselves were getting poorer by the day. The word had got round that they were a bunch of undesirables, and Joe's illness was God's 'judgement' on them. Hysterical mobs gathered at a safe distance from their house – close enough to throw stones but no nearer – trying to make them leave as well. The whole situation was desperate.

Eventually, Joe's mother, Sarah, decided to take a hand. 'Next time Jesus is in the area, we'll get Joe to go and see him,' she said.

'Oh, terrific!' replied her husband. 'That's all we need, some religious nutter mumbling mumbo-jumbo over him. Still, I suppose being laughed at will be better than this!'

Sarah wasn't going to be put off by that kind of talk, and she was as good as her word. You always knew when Jesus was in the area when the religious leaders, who normally wouldn't give each other the time of day, started going around in twos and threes. They were simply terrified of the guy. So when Sarah saw a group of grim-faced parsons in the market square frantically consulting their Bibles, she knew the time had come.

It didn't take long to track Jesus down. She just followed the sound of laughter and cheering, and then she went to the colony and told Joe, 'He'll be staying with his friends in the country, you can be sure, so you can wait for him on the road outside the town.'

Joe was desperate by this time. So that evening he waited as Sarah had said, and sure enough Jesus came along. It took more courage than Joe had ever known he had, to approach Jesus – who grinned broadly when he saw him and held out a hand. Joe shrunk back. 'Don't touch me,' he said, 'I'm unclean, but I know you can cure me if you're willing to.'

Jesus seemed to sense that nothing he said would make Joe feel better as he walked up to him and gently took his horrible, sore-ridden face between his hands. Joe tried to say that it wasn't a good idea – even if he didn't catch anything, Jesus was likely to end up where he was if people heard what he'd done. But he couldn't say anything because he was too busy fighting back the tears. Then he heard the words: 'Of course I'm willing. You're cured.'

Joe and his family never really recovered from the effects of his illness. The old friendships could never be the same, and although the business picked up, it never got back to what it had been. They managed, though, and they knew there was something more important at stake than their wealth.

'One good thing about this,' said Joe's father. 'People might learn to be less hysterical, and not to blame the sufferer.'

Have we learnt it?

PRAYING BIT

Lord,
    what I find frightening
    isn't that other people can react
    and hurt others
    by being judgemental,
    but that *I* can.
And I do.
From small things at school
    to big things in the world.
And I don't even realise I'm doing it.
How awful is that?

I'm not happy about it.
It's not very 'you'.
I'm supposed to love my neighbour
    and follow you.
Bung those together
    and I've got to have unconditional love
    for everyone else.

That's frightening.
It's also exciting,
    and amazing.

Help me, Lord,
    to be unconditional
    in my love.

Amen.

A Pearl of Wisdom

Based on Matthew 13:45-46

THINKING BIT

Even as you read this, there is an army of people out there, plotting to convince you that you need whatever they're selling. And you've really *got* to have the lot. A nice house with a flash car in the drive might impress the neighbours temporarily. But they're going to want to come inside, too. And then you will have to have wall-to-wall shag pile, computer-controlled air conditioning, top-quality furniture and a sound system with all the bells, whistles, woofers and tweeters imaginable and a graphic equaliser for every corner of every room. The satellite dish on the wall outside must be matched by the very latest technology within, and if the TV can do your shopping for you then you just might be considered to measure up. But even all of that will count for nothing if you don't have a well-stocked wine-rack in a kitchen that makes Mission Control look passé.

Of course, you could always be really radical: decide what you really, really want – and what you're willing to give up in order to have it. Now that's *real* 'freedom of choice'.

READING BIT

I wasn't always like this, you know. I had a big house, once – servants, regular entertaining, the whole rig-out. But I had to give it up . . . no, that's not true: I *chose* to give it up. Look, get one of those little folding chairs and sit down and I'll tell you about it. Sorry I've nothing better to sit on, but in a place this size space-saving's important. Oh, and if you're cold I've got some blankets over there – have to be careful about the heating bills, you know. Okay? Comfy? Well, as comfy as you're likely to be anyway?

Right. Well, as I was saying, I didn't always live like this. If you'd come to see me a year ago, I'd have sat you down on a luxurious sofa, given you a glass of the best wine you're ever likely to drink, and had the butler prepare dinner while we talked. But then, life's full of choices, and I've made mine.

I was a merchant, you see, buying and selling pearls. And I was good, make no mistake about it: I could spot the flaw in a near-perfect pearl from ten feet away in a bad light. That's how you get when you're really committed – a true enthusiast. No, not enthusiast – connoisseur. It was a wonderful life, but I was never satisfied. I just knew there must be a really perfect pearl out there somewhere, and although I dealt with the best it never seemed to come my way.

Eventually, I just gave up hoping. I decided I might as well just enjoy my money in other ways. So I bought a bigger house, took on a huge staff of servants and lived the life of Riley (whoever he might have been) with big parties and all the most famous people coming to see me. It was great, but not that great.

Then I got a knock on my door that changed everything. The deputy assistant under-doorman answered it, of course, I never did that kind of thing for myself. He tried to send the guy away, but it was no use. The sound of raised voices filtered through to the conservatory where I was tending the begonias: 'If you value your job, Mush, you'll tell your boss I'm here – or I'll just have to write to him instead, and when he finds out what you turned away you'll be in big trouble. Savvy?'

'If you do not leave,' came the dignified reply, 'I shall be reluctantly compelled to take whatever measures are necessary.'

I didn't like that. By my deputy assistant under-doorman's standards, that's strong language and I knew he was losing his cool. So I went out to see what it was all about.

'A door-to-door salesperson, sir,' explained Barnes, loftily. 'I have acquainted him with your policy of purchasing only from *bona fide* companies of long-standing respectability, but he does not appear to understand.'

'Oh, I understand alright, you brain-dead offspring of an under-achieving camel,' replied the visitor, 'but I'm accustomed to talking to the ringmaster, not his performing flea.'

I had to admit the man had a sort of a way with words, and I'd been wondering for some time what it was I didn't like about Barnes – just couldn't put my finger on it, until now. Even so, however, I wasn't inclined to let this stranger into my house.

'Well, you're talking to him,' I said, 'and he's telling you to go away before he calls security.'

'Suit yourself, friend,' the visitor replied, 'but I've got the one thing you've always wanted.' So saying, he turned away, casually opening his fist as he did so. What I saw made me change my mind about him very quickly.

'Come in, my dear fellow, come in! Barnes, take early retirement. Now, Mr . . . er . . . what did you say your name was?'

'I didn't,' came the taciturn reply. 'Let's say "Joe", shall we?'

After what I'd just seen, I wasn't going to argue about names. And when I got a good look it was even better than I thought. This was a flawless pearl – and I mean flawless. Well, of course, I just had to have it. But Joe drove a hard bargain. 'Five million,' he said.

'Three,' I countered.

'Five million,' he said.

'Three and a half – and an autographed copy of Forster's latest book.'

'Five million,' he said.

'Okay, then – you needn't read the book.'

'Five million, he said.

This was getting boring – and he knew he'd got me, because he'd got the pearl.

'Okay, but I'll need time.'

And that was that. Everything had to go, and now I'm here, living in this shoe-box and watching the pennies. But some things are beyond price, aren't they? Oh, and there's an unexpected spin-off benefit. When I was in my big house, I had to throw a party if I wanted to see anybody. And then they only came for the food or the publicity. Now I'm here I've got neighbours on either side, and they actually seem to like me. We share things, we chat over the fence, we help one another out.

Oh, yes. Some things are definitely worth the sacrifice.

PRAYING BIT

I can't believe it, Lord.
I've done it again.
A little bit of money in my pocket,
    then it's gone.
Well, it's still a little I guess:
    I've got three pence left from the tenner I had earlier.
And nothing to show for it.

Duped again.
Sucked in by sparkly shop windows,
    colourful colourfulness
    and adverts that work.
I'm almost ashamed.

So there I was,
    bag full of things I'd bought
    but didn't know why,
    leaving the shop,
    and I happened to pass someone
    asking for money.

They looked pretty homeless
    but I had nothing to give,
    except this three pence.
And I felt too guilty to only give that.
Not right, is it, Lord?

Next time,
    when I'm out
    and the adverts are whispering,
    help me to hear the whispers of others
    who need my money
    more than I needed this T-shirt.

Amen.

Law Versus Prophet

Based on Mark 3:1-6

THINKING BIT

Oh, so you think the Pharisees were only around in Jesus' time, do you? Take a look around. They're alive and kicking the Christian church to death. I doubt there's a street in Britain where you wouldn't find one: someone who thinks Christianity is all about balancing the books with God – getting it right, being respectable, keeping the rules.

And the real tragedy with such people is that they're good people – just like the original Pharisees – who are simply unable to accept the idea of unconditional love.

READING BIT

Confidential Memo

From: Simon, Senior Pharisee
To: The General Secretary, The Herodian party

Right, so whose clever idea was it to try and trap that Jesus and discredit him? I said at the last council meeting it wouldn't work, but I was totally shouted down. 'He's a slippery customer,' I told you all. 'He'll find a way of turning the tables.' But would anybody listen? I want it on record that I followed the plan to the letter. It's not my fault it failed; I always knew it would.

The time has now come for drastic action. I don't care how you do it – just keep Jesus away from my synagogue. I've devoted my entire career as a Pharisee to keeping the congregation on track for harps, haloes and hallelujahs and I don't want him messing up my good record. We've been top of the league tables in every category (Piety, Pedantry and Pastoral Care) for the past five years, and I intend that it should stay that way. In the past we've always been able to deal quickly with any rebellious types; it's just a matter of pulling a bit of rank and putting the fear of God into them.

Then along came Jesus and undid it all in no time flat. To begin with, they listen to him more than they do to me – so much for the 'rank' bit – and then he tells them they don't need to be afraid of God. God, it seems, loves everybody, whether they're good or not. He loves con-merchants, prostitutes, Romans, Samaritans – absolutely no standards whatever. It's getting to the stage where I can't control my own congregation, and God help society when religious leaders can't control their congregations.

Of course, I admit our plan was good in theory: if the people could see Jesus openly flouting the law he'd lose his aisle credibility – after all, most synagogue people are law-abiding – and then he'd be no threat. So my instructions were to set up a situation Jesus wouldn't be able to resist, and I knew just what that was: an opportunity to heal somebody, even if it was the sabbath and it was illegal to work. (I can't see the fascination myself; I mean, when you've seen one healthy body you've seen them all, but there you go.)

There was nothing wrong with the way I carried out my plan. As it happened, I knew just the person to use as bait: a chap called Ben who's been begging at the end of our street for years. He's got this horrible, grotesque hand – looks a bit like a withered branch on a tree – and he's always saying he'd give anything to have it put right. So I invited him to the synagogue. Normally, of course, I'd have discouraged the likes of him. People like that in the synagogue put the punters off their prayers. But this was a special circumstance. I put Ben in a prominent place, right where I knew Jesus would see him.

To be fair, it nearly worked. Jesus took the bait as soon as he came in – called Ben out and stood him in full view of everybody. But as soon as he opened his mouth I knew I'd been right. He's got the gift of the gab, has Jesus, and I knew he'd wriggle out of it, which he did.

He asked the people, 'Is it permitted to do good on the sabbath or to do evil? To save life, or to kill?'

Of course, it was a false question. The law doesn't say you

should do evil on the sabbath, just that you shouldn't actually do good. There's a big difference, as any lawyer will tell you, but of course Jesus knows that the people aren't legally trained. And given that choice, there wasn't much anybody could say. I just had to stand there in horrible silence, waiting for the inevitable.

Jesus didn't act at once. He just stood there, looking at me, as if to say, 'You stupid, obstinate old Pharisee' and defying me to argue with him. Well, as I said, it was a catch question; he's good at those, and they're his standard way of avoiding clear-cut legal issues.

Eventually, he turned to Ben and said, 'Stretch out your hand.' What happened next fully vindicated my policy of keeping people like Ben away from the synagogue. If he'd had any nous, he'd just have kept his arm still – cracked on he couldn't use it – but oh no, he has to do as Jesus asks. And suddenly that arm was as good as the other one and everyone was yelling and cheering enough to bring the roof down.

Okay, so what was I supposed to do? Perhaps now someone will listen to me. Subtlety is not the way to deal with Jesus: like all dangerous radicals he's too clever for that. He's got to be got rid of. I don't know whether you are fully aware of the gravity of the situation: if people once take on board Jesus' teachings and actually live by them, it would be the end of all we hold dear.

There can now only be one course of action open to us: kill him – in the national interest, of course.

PRAYING BIT

Unconditional love is an amazing thing.
By its very nature it crosses over everything
   and still exists.
You can ignore it,
   insult it,
   do bad against it,
   try and kill it,
   but it's still there
   and it's still loving you;
   unconditionally.

So why do people (including me, Lord) find it so hard
   to understand?
Simple; they (we) want unconditional love
   with conditions.

We want to preach about it
   but not have to love someone who's gay.
We want to believe in it
   so long as we don't have to hug that bloke who committed
   murder.
We want to sell it
   as long as we are safe in the knowledge that some people
   will never, ever, get into heaven.

Not exactly unconditional.
Not exactly 'died on the cross' love.
But that's us, Lord, and some of us are trying to get it right.

Love us all, Lord,
   regardless of what we are,
   with your unconditional love.

Amen.

Power Without Politics

Based on Mark 5:22-43

THINKING BIT

It's tough at the top – and toughest of all is when being at the top makes no difference: all the string-pulling, palm-greasing and general power-play that's an everyday part of life suddenly counts for about as much as a lucky horse-shoe at a wake.

That's the thing about Death – he can't be bribed, he's seldom cheated and his decision is usually final. He'd make a rotten politician.

READING BIT

Funny how you can take life for granted. It just never occurred to me that there was any problem I couldn't solve. When you're the president of the synagogue you get used to having power and influence. People are very eager to please:

'Anything I can do for you, Jairus?'

'Come to dinner, sometime, Jairus?'

'Here, let me carry that for you, Jairus.'

And if ever I was in any difficulty – like if I'd got my tax wrong or something – I could usually find someone to sort it out for me, and all without looking beyond my usual circle of friends. Then something happened that no amount of money or political influence could change – and I was absolutely lost.

'Hey, Jairus! Come and look at Sarah.'

My wife Sue's voice had that anxious edge to it that always made me nervous. Something was wrong. I followed the sound into Sarah's bedroom and saw at once why she was worried. Sarah was still in bed, when any self-respecting 12-year-old should have been up and at it, either playing with her friends or showing her appreciation of the expensive gadgets and gizmos that all well-to-do parents buy their children.

But she wasn't. She was just lying there in bed, with her eyes closed and her breathing sounding more like a horse after a chariot race than a well-brought-up debutante.

Well, I wasted no time. 'Send for Dr. Amos!' I said. 'He'll cure her – if he ever wants to practise around here again.'

Luckily, Sue was a bit more level-headed than I was at that moment. 'Now, don't go pulling rank on him,' she said. 'It offends his professional pride, and anyway you know he'll do all he can, without being threatened.'

She was right, but it didn't stop me worrying. And I got even more worried when Dr. Amos arrived, took one look at Sarah and put on his 'prophet of doom' face. 'It's no good,' he said. 'I'm afraid you'll have to prepare yourself for the worst.'

By now I'd just about lost it – I'd always said if anything happened to Sarah I'd go out of my mind. 'Send for a specialist!' I cried. 'Get me someone who knows what he's talking about.'

Dr. Amos shook his head. 'Even if a specialist could help we'd never get one here in time.' As he said it, he kindly returned the bag of money I'd just shoved into his hand. 'Come on now, Jairus, you know if I could cure her I would, without bribes.'

Sue took me outside and spoke quietly but firmly. 'D'you think I'm not as devastated as you? We've got to keep cool and think – at least she's alive at the moment, and at the very least let's not make these last hours worse than they need be. I think we should send for Jesus.'

Obviously, I wasn't the only one who'd lost it. Jesus, for the record, was an untrained, even uneducated, itinerant preacher and healer who'd only been around for five minutes but had succeeded in upsetting every synagogue president in the area. The people loved him because he seemed to say that God's love was free, so naturally he became a magnet for every weirdo and ne'er-do-well around.

'I can't ask him!' I said. 'I'd never hold my head up in the synagogue again.'

Sue didn't need to say anything. It was my own words that brought me up short. My life! Had I really said that? Normally, it would have been right – most of us proper clergy wouldn't be seen giving Jesus the time of day. But when your daughter's life is on the line, pride doesn't seem so important. So I set out.

Jesus wasn't difficult to find – there always seemed to be a huge, noisy rabble around him wherever he went. They let me through, though, because they all knew who I was. All of a sudden, I really appreciated the respect and affection they had for me, and realised how much I'd taken it for granted before. Well, whatever happened next, I decided I was going to learn my lesson about that.

When I got to Jesus, I couldn't believe what I found myself doing. In my position you normally try to preserve at least a semblance of dignity, but before I knew it I was down at the feet of this disreputable tramp, blubbing like a baby and begging him to come and heal Sarah. He didn't say anything. Just took my arm, lifted me up and followed where I led. It was very impressive. Not flamboyant, just impressive.

We'd hardly gone five paces when he was interrupted. I'll tell you the full story another time, but suffice it to say it gave me the heebie-jeebies. He behaved as if he had all the time in the world, stopping to help this woman with a haemorrhage. Looking back, I realise it was an impressive example of compassion and self-confidence – the kind that only comes from having real power, not my kind; but at the time, well, they were the longest two minutes of my life. Just as he was finishing, Barney, my secretary, arrived.

'Sorry, sir,' he said. 'It's too late; don't bother Jesus about it.'

Jesus overheard, and said, 'Don't worry, Jairus, have faith.'

For some strange reason, I did – although from anyone else that sort of talk wouldn't have helped. We carried on and got to the house. The professional mourners were there and you could hear the weeping and wailing from yards away. Jesus gave them short shrift: 'Oh, stop your caterwauling! She's not dead, just asleep.'

That got him a scornful laugh from the Chief Wailer; he'd seen enough of death to recognise it when he saw it. But we got everyone out and took Jesus into Sarah's room. He went over to her bed and took her hand. She looked pretty dead to me, I have to say, but Jesus just said, 'Come on, my child, get up.'

'My child'! Only Jesus could have got away with that. Sarah was coming up to marriageable age and proud of it. But she just opened her eyes, smiled and got up. I fell apart again, trying to get him to accept payment, return favours, all that kind of thing. But of course when you've got that sort of power, you don't need my kind of wealth and influence, do you?

PRAYING BIT

Lord,
   this whole death thing . . .
   bit scary really.
I've been told I'm supposed to be 'unafraid'
   because I'm a Christian.
Well, stuff that.
Death frightens me – to death.

I don't want to die.
I don't want to experience the pain.
I imagine it all,
   I have nightmares about how I'll die!
It's not nice, Lord!

Sorry.
Very morbid, I know,
   but it's a difficult thing to get away from.

What was it like, Lord?
Dying?
Don't answer.

Oh, Lord,
I don't know what this is about.
Just fear I guess;
   like the monsters under the bed.
All very real to me.
I hope you understand.

Amen.

Sorry to Interrupt

Based on Mark 5:25-34

THINKING BIT

Just touch the edge – that's what we do when we're afraid. Just touch the edge of life, of society, of the church . . .

For some people, that's all they feel able to do, especially if they have a condition that makes them 'unclean' in society's eyes. In a society obsessed with 'standards', it's hardly surprising that some people feel the only part of the 'body of Christ' they can touch is the edge of the garment.

READING BIT

I didn't mean to interrupt – honestly – I could see he was busy. Jesus had just got this urgent call from someone whose daughter was dying, and the last thing I wanted to do was to get in the way. Especially as the person concerned was Jairus, who's one of the clergy – I mean, they have to have priority don't they, important people like that. Anyway, I knew my place; I've always made a point of knowing my place. It gets a bit lonely sometimes, always being on the edge of everything, but you get used to it – especially when you've got a disease like mine. Family? What family? They'd gone long ago. Well, it's a man's world round here and mine decided to find another – world and wife, that is – ages ago.

My friend Rachel had this thing about getting me healed. She reckoned Jesus could do it, but I said he's not for the likes of me. Anyway, she pestered and pestered until I thought I'd better go and see him if only for a bit of peace! You'll never know how much effort it took to screw up my courage. I was just about to go and have a word when Jairus arrived. Well, it's like I said; I couldn't interrupt that. But I knew it would be weeks before I'd be able to psych myself up again, so I had to do something.

'Well,' I thought, 'if he's as good as he's cracked up to be then I don't need to ask him. I bet if I just touched the edge of his coat I'd get the healing from that. I mean, they say he's just full of it – healing power oozing out of every pore in his body.' So before I could think it through and change my mind, I crept towards him.

He was just starting out for Jairus's house, and the crowd was pushing closer; they obviously knew something terrific was in the air. So I reached out, and as soon as I made contact with his coat I felt better. Suddenly I had energy again! I could have crushed a ripe tomato with one hand! Okay, so it's no big deal to you, but it shows you how I felt before.

Anyway, I turned round and tried to get away, but I was too late. Jesus stopped. The crowd didn't. It was a bit like the domino effect. (What's a domino?) Everyone just piled into everyone else and it was chaos. Then Jesus asked, 'Who touched me?'

Some people thought that was funny – enough people around him to fill an amphitheatre and he was asking who touched him! Jairus didn't seem amused, though, and I can fully sympathise. His daughter was at the point of death and Jesus was stopping to ask questions like that! I tried to slip away. I'd got what I wanted, and didn't see any point in drawing attention to myself, but I couldn't get through the crush of people. Everybody started yelling at him to forget it, but he wouldn't; he just stood there wanting to know who'd touched him. I thought I must have done something really dreadful – should have known my place, you see, and kept away. Now this really important person was being inconvenienced and a lovely child was being put in danger, all because I'd got above myself.

Well, he carried on asking – and Jairus was finding it more and more difficult to look patient – and it was obvious nothing was going to change until I'd owned up. Well, I couldn't have the death of that little girl on my conscience, could I? So I did what I'm best at. I grovelled. Seriously grovelled. Down on my knees, all the hand-wringing, weeping and wailing to go with it. 'I'm terribly sorry – really sorry – didn't mean any harm – won't do it again – just ignore me – go to Jairus's house. Honestly, I'm really, really sorry.'

I braced myself, kept my eyes closed, waited for the eruption. Nothing happened.

Then I heard Jesus speak again. 'Why didn't you just ask? What were you afraid of?'

I thought it must be a wind-up. Any time now, he was going to show me exactly what I should have been afraid of. And if he didn't, then Jairus would – especially if his daughter died because I'd got in the way. All my life I'd developed only one talent – keeping out of the way – and I did it to perfection. So why did I have to choose this precise moment to muck it all up?

Suddenly I felt this hand taking my arm. That was it, then; I was going to get dragged back to the edge of the town where I belonged. But no, he was ever so gentle, just lifted me up and made me look into his face.

'That took a lot of courage,' he said. 'And faith. Well, because of that you're healed. Now stop apologising for breathing, and go and get a life, preferably a good one. You deserve it.'

I was absolutely gobsmacked, I don't mind saying. I could hardly make out anything because my eyes were full of tears, but what I couldn't miss was Jairus, still standing there, trying to look patient bless him, and no doubt going through agonies. So I didn't hang about. Somehow I found the energy to get through the crowd and out the other side, and I just kept going.

It all worked out well in the end, though. I heard later that Jairus's daughter was okay, in fact I've seen her around since, and she's never looked better. Me too, actually. The sickness has gone, I'm a lot nicer to know, and I've got some real prospects. Everything's coming together for me now. But you know the best thing: confidence! It wasn't the illness, but what it made me feel about myself. Well, that's all changed.

Watch out world – here I come!

PRAYING BIT

That's faith, Lord;
   to know she could be healed just by touching your cloak.
Amazing.
I sometimes feel I have a faith like that.
But it's only sometimes, Lord.
Most of the time
   I question everything I do,
   everything I think,
   everything I believe.
There's nothing wrong with questions
   but they can take over.
And they do.

I forget what I'm about,
   what you're about.
I get swept up by the world,
   by its cynicism,
   by its obsessions.
I become like everyone else,
   when the whole point
   is that I'm not like everyone else.

And the crowd can be so crushing,
   sweeping me under,
   as I desperately try
   to keep my eye on you.

Help me reach out to you, Lord,
   and touch your cloak.

Amen.

Dance, Salome, Dance!

Based on Mark 6:17-29, 14-16

THINKING BIT

Some folk never learn. You don't have to stop as recently as this story. Go back and back through history and the lesson's there for all to see: threatening, manipulating or even killing people of principle doesn't work. Prophets are like London buses – there'll be another one along in a few minutes.

READING BIT

I should never have listened to my mother.

'Salome,' she used to say, 'with a body like yours, you could have anything you want.'

Well, she should know, she'd done pretty well for herself. Whatever *she* wanted had included my Dad's brother, who just happened to be King Herod of Judea. In a land where women generally counted for a bit less than the dust of the streets, she'd clawed her way to the top – and Herod had the scratches on his back to prove it. But was she happy? Not a bit of it.

There was this other guy, see . . . oh, nothing like that, though. This one had more sense. John the Baptist, he was called. He was one of those Jewish prophets – all fiery eyes and wild speeches – quite attractive in a primitive sort of way, but not my type. He'd got this sort of water fetish, and as for his idea of a good home-cooked romantic dinner . . . well, you wouldn't believe it if I told you. Anyway, he'd really got it in for my mother in a big way. Listen, and you'll see what I mean.

'Woe! Woe! An abomination to the Lord! For doth not the Good Book say, "Thou shalt not marry thy brother's wife"? King Herod is a sinner and his wife is a whore. And the Lord will punish the sinner; the whore shall burn for eternity . . .'

Yeah, yeah, we've heard it before – cliché night at St Walter's in the Wilderness. Nothing particularly startling there, I'd have thought. I guess he might have got away with that stuff if he hadn't gone on: 'A Jezebel, I say, a common, painted Jezebel!' Now if you want my opinion, it was the 'common' bit that did it. Mother never had any standards but she did have her pride. Anyway, before he could say 'This is the word of the Lord', he was banged up in a cell with only the rats to rant at.

If you ask me, I reckon old King Hairdo was just a touch afraid of him. I don't think he'd have arrested him if Mother hadn't threatened to ask for her dowry back – kept mumbling things about not wanting to turn a fanatic into a folk-hero. Then, once John was safely in the cell, I think he hoped that mother would shut up, but no such luck.

The big crunch came when Herod had this party; all sorts of people came along to drink his wine, eat his food and butter him up – and you know what that means, don't you: before long, someone's going to have to entertain them. So along comes Mother with one of her Big Ideas. 'Why don't you go and dance for them?' she said, 'After all, with a body like yours . . .'

I didn't wait. I knew the rest of the speech – and I also knew there was no point in arguing. If dancing in front a bunch of smug, self-obsessed, boring old wind-breaks was what I had to do . . . well anyway, it was better than what Mother had had to do to get on. So I went and got the veils.

I tell you, it's demeaning! All the creativity, the artistry, the long, painful hours of dedicated practice, the commitment to interpretive integrity – and all they really wanted was a peep show. But one day I'm going to get to the top in legit. theatre; I'd like to be a serious Oscar, win an actor and tell everybody I'm committed to world peace and animal rights. But that's all for later. Right now, I've got a greasy pole to climb. So there I was, winking, wiggling, and wobbling in all the right places to the sound of this wheezy old flute and trying not to think about what the audience might be thinking about.

Eventually, the flute player died of asphyxiation and I could stop – and that's when old King Hernia made his great offer. He was sitting there, sweating like it was his last chance, with a big silly grin on his face and yelling, 'Encore!' (pretentious little so-and-so, just because he'd once read half-way through a travel brochure before he realised it wasn't a comic) and saying silly things like 'More! More! My kingdom for some more!'

Well, to cut a long story short – and someone's got to – old Herod meant what he said, well, half of it, which is better than his usual track record.

'Half my kingdom!' he ranted. 'Whatever you want, up to half my kingdom!'

Now, I knew exactly what I wanted: an introduction to a top director at the Coliseum, a water-tight contract, a part in the next block buster and a guarantee on residuals. What I ended up with was quite another matter – thanks to Mother.

'Tell him you want the head of John the Baptist,' she hissed. Well, perhaps I should have asked for time to think it over, but you know how sometimes these things happen. I saw the old lecher sitting there grinning at me, and I just snapped. It was the last thing he'd want to give me, and if I'm honest I never thought he'd do it. I just wanted to make him squirm a bit.

'Right,' I heard myself saying. 'The head of John the Baptist. And why not put it on a nice silver salver while you're at it!'

Herod squirmed alright – tried everything – but Mother wasn't going to let him off the hook. I suppose I should have expected that. 'You promised,' she shrieked over and over again, and eventually he gave in. Have you ever tried to look pleased when someone presents you with a disembodied head, still warm and with the eyes still rolling, on a silver platter? No? Let's just say it proved once and for all my calibre as an actor.

My big chance, and I stuffed it up! Still, I might yet get another. There's this new guy on the block, called Jesus. He's getting up Mother's nose as well, and he's got Herod well scared because he thinks John the Baptist has come back to life. Neither Herod nor Mother has slept a wink in a week, and this time it's got nothing to do with her clawing her way to the top.

What do I think? I don't know. I'm a thespian, not a philosopher. But I'm thinking of opening a shop specialising in gruesome wig stands.

PRAYING BIT

Not nice that;
   having your head lopped off
   and served up as a Sunday lunch.
Then old Herod gets worried
   that you've come back.

Prophets have a habit of getting killed, Lord.
Or at least having something horrible happen to them.

Even today,
   someone stands up,
   speaks the truth about injustice,
   and bingo:
   a bullet to the brain –
   or something.

But before you know it,
   someone else is there.
And another,
   and another.

And they're all slammed in prison.

The world seems to hate having the mirror
   thrust in its face.
The grime's obvious and ugly.
Best to smash the mirror
   or hide it and hope everyone forgets it was ever there.

But the grime won't budge
   and the reflection stays the same.
Be with them, Lord:
   your people persecuted.

Amen.

Too Good for Words

Based on Luke 1:5-25, 57-66

THINKING BIT

Have you noticed that almost all of Luke's gospel is in brackets? Only figuratively speaking, of course. The opening 'bracket' is a story that brings two marginalised women to the centre of a generally patriarchal faith. The closing 'bracket' places faithful women at the very heart of the resurrection story. Seen between those brackets, the Gospel according to Luke takes on a fresh and exciting character – but let's begin at the beginning.

READING BIT

Dear Bishop,

I'm writing to set the record straight about the scurrilous rumours that have been going round. I would not like you to be in any doubt about either my faith or the stability of my marriage (and my writing this has nothing at all to do with the fact that the archdeacon is about to retire and leave his post vacant).

This has been a traumatic experience for me, but my therapist believes I've made excellent progress and that my long-term career prospects should not be affected by the incident.

For the record: it is quite true that I did not speak to my wife or my parishioners for nine months; it is not true that I have been hallucinating or that I have lost my faith. The suggestion that my mental state is unstable is a vicious rumour put out by people who are out to get me.

I was getting ready to start worship – I'd got a cracker of a sermon ready – when suddenly an angel appeared: all decked out in his best jeans and T-shirt, with 'To Gaby from John Lennon' autographed on his guitar, a designer halo on his head, and bits of fluffy cloud on his trainers. That was my first lesson – God doesn't work in stereotypes.

I was terrified at first, and not only because I thought he might want to start youth services or something, just that it was a really strange experience.

Anyway, he took off his shades, looked me in the eye, and said, 'Congratulations, Zack, you're going to be a daddy. So learn your nappy drill and open an account at Smothercare. Oh, and by the way, the baby's got to be named John; it's about time your family got a bit of street cred. He'll be a cool dude – you're overdue for one of those in your line, as well – and he'll start a religious revival like you've never known. Don't worry, nothing happy clappy, just a good old-fashioned guilt-trip with lots of repentance and that sort of thing. Okay?'

Now, if I'm honest, I don't think my reaction was unreasonable. I mean, Elizabeth and I aren't getting any younger, and she couldn't conceive for love or money, even before she lost her youth, looks and inclination. Honestly, I wasn't calling him a liar, just perhaps a bit mistaken, maybe carried away by all that flower-power stuff, who knows? But he took it personally and got really huffy.

'This is me you're talking to,' he sniffed, 'Gabriel: archangel, heavenly body and celestial fashion guru, not to mention honorary musical director of the Choir Invisible. I've put up with some things down the ages, but no one's ever accused me of terminological inexactitudes before.' Then, seeing my puzzled look, he added, 'What's the matter? Cat got your tongue? Now there's an idea! We'll leave it that way for a while and give your wife a bit of peace. Perhaps after the kid's been born you might have something worthwhile to say, so I'll review your case then.'

And before I could write him a note of retraction and apology, he'd gone, leaving behind only a whiff of Heavenly Spice body lotion and a jangling guitar chord that even John Lennon himself – whoever he might be – could never have thought of.

I don't mind telling you, the pregnancy was very difficult, really painful and demoralising. I never want to go through that again as long as I live. I mean, the whole time I wasn't able to say anything at all, and I even had to go back to college and do an NVQ in Non-verbal Communication just so I could communicate with my own wife. Well, there are some things you don't want to put into writing, aren't there? And all the time I had to live with this stigma – a priest being struck dumb for lack of faith. Just because everyone expects clergy to be full of fiery conviction and never to have any doubts, it made me a laughing stock. And there was worse to come.

When the baby was born, they were all over us – the parishioners, that is – treating Elizabeth like a celebrity and me like an irrelevance just because I couldn't speak. Then they all started going on about names, and I knew it was going to get worse. 'His name's John,' Elizabeth told them.

'Oh, surely not? I mean, you've got to name him after his Dad. Don't you think *poor, dear* Zack has been humiliated enough?'

I developed a permanent cringe around that period. I thought that at any moment they were going to start patting me on the head and sending cards with pious texts on them saying they were sure God still loved me. I had to put an end to it and, eventually, I managed to get them to give me a pen and paper. I wrote on it in big letters, 'His name is John, and that's that.'

'There we are,' shouted some wag, 'Now he's put it in writing!' For me, it was the final insult. Elizabeth had been centre-stage all the way through, and now I was completely sidelined. I think anyone would have found that strain a little too much to cope with.

However, I'm glad to report that I'm now fully recovered. My speech returned immediately, my therapist has sent a discharge letter to my doctor, and I've been declared fully fit for work.

That, my dear Bishop, is a full and true account of the events. While I'm writing, perhaps you and your good wife would like to call in for dinner one evening – we'd love to entertain you. Any time would suit us, but perhaps before you get too busy with the meetings and interviews about the choice of the new archdeacon?

Yours in his love,
Zechariah.

PRAYING BIT

Well, theatrics again, Lord, by the look of things.
Someone unable to have a baby
    having one.
Someone losing a voice
    because they didn't believe it was possible.

Very 'you' indeed.

It strikes me as odd
    that sometimes you like the subtle approach
    and then opt for something really out of the ordinary.
Why is that?

I don't need an answer.

Why do I ask, though?
Well, I'm pretty ordinary
    and I wouldn't mind something theatrical and extraordinary
    happening to me.
Is that OK?
It's not a request or a demand;
    just a thought.

Thanks for listening.

Amen.

Quite Contrary

Based on Luke 1:26-56

THINKING BIT

It's interesting, don't you think, this 'a virgin shall conceive' thing? Mary lived in a patriarchal society where women were generally considered rather less use than ornaments – until they were in a position to start producing children, which by definition virgins weren't. So it followed that, even in this respect women on their own could achieve nothing. That is why Mary was later able to sing the powerful words of the Magnificat. The humble had truly been lifted high.

READING BIT

I tell you, it's true. I'm a good girl, I am, and I don't tell whoppers. I never asked for all of this to happen. I was having a nice restful day at home, knocking out the wall for a kitchen extension – the way you do – when I heard this amazing voice, singing. The lyrics were a bit unoriginal, but the music was, well . . . out of this world, really, sort of . . . futuristic:

'All you need is God, God,
God is all you need.'

Oh dear,' I thought, 'another angel. There goes my little bit of relaxation.' God's got this habit of sending angels – messengers – to tell people things. Now, a lot of people don't recognise them because they're expecting long flowing robes, harps, haloes and homely countenances. But some of us know better. It's difficult to describe what makes angels different, but if your mind's open you recognise them. Anyway, where was I? Yes, this angel.

'Greetings, Mary,' he sort of intoned, 'the Lord has really *blessed* you.'

'Oh, cut the piety and get to the point,' I said. These hippie,

God-squad types really irritate me.

'Oh, alright, just trying to keep ahead of the times,' he apologised. 'Anyway, God's chosen you – you're really honoured – you're going to have a baby, the Son of God.'

This sounded a bit strange to me, but Gabriel was obviously quite carried away by the idea. He started strumming his guitar and crooned:

'You're going to have a baby,
he's going to be God's Son,
all people will adore him,
(adore him, adore him)
the High and Mighty One.

The Lord will make him mighty,
he'll sit on David's throne,
and he will reign for ever,
(for ever, for ever)
and no end to his rule shall ever be known.'

He looked sad. 'You know, I've been working on that last line for a good ten minutes, but I just can't make it scan.'

'Never mind,' I soothed, 'It's all over now.' And a jolly good thing, too – I know God's pretty open-minded, but singing telegrams are taking things a bit far, don't you think?

As he looked like having another go, I interrupted hastily. 'Why not just tell me the message?'

Gabriel looked hurt. 'Okay, then – you're going to have a baby, and he'll be known as God's Son, and he'll reign for ever on the throne of David.'

'Oh, right,' I answered. 'Why didn't you just say so?' Then a thought struck me. 'Hang on a minute, I haven't got a husband, and you know what they say about twosomes and tangos.'

Gabriel groaned. 'Don't get into that,' he said. 'I've only just mastered the Charleston. But if you mean what I *think* you mean, don't worry. God's going to take care of everything, and contrary to popular opinion *he's* the centre of the universe.'

'Matter of fact,' Gabriel went on, his face lighting up as though he'd just invented boil-in-the-bag poached salmon, 'You know your cousin Elizabeth – the one everyone said couldn't conceive short of a miracle?'

'Well it would take one now,' I answered flatly. 'She's no spring chicken, you know.'

'Chicken? Chicken? Whoever mentioned chickens?'

That's the trouble with people who live in the clouds, they can be a bit unworldly. 'Oh, never mind, I said, 'just that she's not young.'

'Oh! Right! Gotcha. Well, that just goes to show. She's pregnant – has been for nearly six months – so if you're talking of miracles . . . '

I didn't hear much more – suddenly there were more urgent things to do than gossip.

'Fine,' I said. 'Sure! Just tell God, he's the boss, so whatever he wants, I'm in. Okay?' With that, I gathered up my strength, my skirts and a few eggs for a present and set off at the trot.

It was true! Elizabeth and I just laughed and laughed for joy! We had a lot in common, when you think about it. For different reasons, we were both pretty unlikely mothers, but God had chosen us for two of the most important roles in his purpose.

Talk about turning the world upside down!

PRAYING BIT

There you go again!
Theatrics,
    making an impression,
    doing things differently.
Mary must have been pretty shocked,
    and as for poor Joseph . . .

Wonder what that must have been like;
    to be the 'parents' of God's son.
A little bit of pressure, you'd think.

I often wonder how my parents feel.
I'm no 'God's son' that's for sure,
    but I guess I'm pretty special.
I'm here for a start,
    and that's quite something.
I can breathe,
    I can live,
    I can make a difference.

So perhaps,
    with a bit of divine intervention,
    something great
    can come from my humble beginnings?

Help me see outside the stable, Lord.

Amen.

No Room (For the Likes of You)

Based on Luke 2:1-7

THINKING BIT

Strange, the assumptions we make. The Bible never mentions a stable, but we've got it firmly into our heads that that's where Jesus was born. No 'inn', either. The word should be translated as 'guest room', suggesting they were actually staying in a private house – most probably with relatives. So, we may ask, why was the guest room unavailable to a relative who was nine months pregnant?

Could it be that scandal and shame had already begun to gather around him who was to be derided as the 'friend of sinners' – that he was 'numbered amongst the transgressors' even before he was born? In other words, did he begin life by identifying with people who, two millennia later, are still stigmatised in respectable society? What follows is my speculation, although an informed one, and the reader may want to reject it entirely. However, accurate or not, historically speaking, it deepens the wonder of the Incarnation. 'He came to his own, and his own did not receive him.'

READING BIT

Let's get this straight, I'm as loyal to my family as the next person, but you've got to have some standards. When my brother Joseph married that Mary, we all knew there was something not quite right about it. He actually told me, later, that he had considered dumping her (quietly, of course; he's a compassionate man, my brother, and he wouldn't have wanted to hurt her more than necessary) but he decided against it because he said it was God's will. Now, it's not that I'm lacking faith or anything, but saying that God's the father of your baby isn't faith, it's blasphemy, and that's something else we won't have in our household.

Anyway, I always said Joseph would be welcome any time, but I wasn't having that Mary of his under my roof, not in that condition, anyway. Then, what happens? Some barmpot of a civil servant goes and suggests a census, and suddenly Joseph's back in Bethlehem, wife and unborn child and all, needing somewhere to stay.

Well, I'm nothing if not forgiving, and you can't see a pregnant woman out on the street, can you, so of course I let them stay. Not in the guest room, mind you – they weren't the only members of our family who'd suddenly descended on us, you know, and I was relieved to be able to tell them that the guest room was occupied. Well, it sounded nicer than, 'You aren't having that in my spare room,' and it wasn't exactly a lie. I compromised, being the kind soul that I am, and let her have the baby where the animals were sheltered for the night. She'd get plenty of warmth from all that bovine body heat, and I knew they'd have enough clean straw. So that's what they did, and they seemed happy enough.

I told Joseph he didn't need to stay there, but could come inside if he wanted to – after all, he was the wronged party as far as I could see – but he was determined to be with Mary. That's my family, you see, loyal to a fault.

It wasn't long before they had visitors. I tell you, I don't know what Mary sees in people like that. They must have been known to her, because they certainly aren't acquainted with any of *my* family. Shepherds! I ask you! They lead their flocks everywhere and anywhere looking for pasture; no respect for the private property we respectable folks have worked hard to pay for, and they're the most dirty people you ever imagined.

Now, I'm no prude, but I know what shepherds do when sheep are having trouble lambing, and I don't want any hands that have been where theirs have, running along *my* mantelpiece checking for dust, thank you very much. Apart from anything else, we'd have to have the whole place and ourselves ritually purified before we could go near the synagogue again, and you know how gossip spreads . . . if that ever got out, we'd have to move. No, I mean it – we'd simply have to move.

Now, where was I? Oh, yes: shepherds – just came waltzing

in as though they owned the place, no doubt bringing the usual contingent of uninvited livestock that inhabit such people. And as soon as they opened their mouths, I knew there was something funny going on, and they were obviously friends of Mary's – they'd got a 'God' story, as well. Oh, they didn't actually say 'virginal conception' – no, that would have been *so* obvious, and they were clearly much too clever for that. They talked about a special baby, sent by God (which obviously amounts to the same thing) and said an angel had told them all about it. Yes, honestly! And not just one angel, but apparently there were hosts of them, all singing and dancing enough to wake the dead, and at a time when decent people were sleeping.

And had these angels appeared to anyone else? Did we get visits from priests, or from rabbis? No. Of course we didn't: the whole thing was patently obviously a story they'd cooked up between them. I was having none of it.

'You can see her out there,' I said to them, 'but if you think you're coming in here, you can think again. I keep a respectable house, I do.'

They said they'd got proof that this baby was special. How else would they have known about the manger and the swaddling clothes, they said. Yes, well, I wasn't born yesterday.

Yet again, I tried to warn Joseph: 'That child's trouble,' I told him, 'and no one would blame you if you divorced that Mary and tried again with a nice, conventional girl. The daughter of the local butcher is very sought-after. I'm sure I could arrange a match.' But no, Joseph insisted that this was all part of God's great scheme to liberate his people. 'We can do without that kind of talk for a start,' I told him. 'Walls have ears, you know.'

I was right, too. That was 30 years ago, and Jesus is nothing but trouble. He's left the family business to go and be a wandering preacher, with a bunch of ne'er-do-wells that suit him down to the ground. And he's completely disrespectful toward the priests and the Pharisees – always seems to think he knows better. I mean, I'm nothing if not compassionate, but if the religious authorities say that lepers and Samaritans are unclean, who is he to say differently? I tell you, he's going to come to a sticky end one day, and I'm only relieved that Joseph, God rest him, isn't still here to see it.

Son of God, indeed! The only consolation is that it's our side of the family that'll go down in history (my kosher cream teas in aid of synagogue funds are renowned throughout Judea) and Mary and her lot will be forgotten in no time.

Just you wait and see.

PRAYING BIT

Well, there's a turn up for the books.
All this time I've thought it was an inn
    and now perhaps I think it wasn't.
Turned away from the guest room . . .
    now that's plain rude.

But then, if Joseph was going to his 'home town',
    I never could quite understand
    why he tried to stay in a pub.
Surely he had family there?
Anyway, what it brings home
    is the world into which you were born;
    a world rejecting you from the beginning.
And you were only a baby!
They hadn't seen anything yet!
Then Herod gets all worked up
    and tries to kill you.
You attracted trouble, that's for sure.

But for what?
Turning the tables over, that's what.
The tables not just in the temple
    but in people's lives.
Their ideologies, their beliefs,
    their weaknesses,
    their misconceptions . . .
    all thrown onto the floor and scattered
    by you.

Amazing.
Help me turn a few tables over, Lord.

Amen.

The Devil of a Job

Based Luke 4:1-13

THINKING BIT

'Well, if we're God's special people, why shouldn't we get something out of it? Nothing wrong with a few perks, is there? And anyone with any political sense knows you have to compromise, don't they? So pull a publicity stunt or two, get the punters interested, and what's good for us will eventually be good for God.'

Tempting, isn't it!

READING BIT

Okay, I don't mind admitting it: we were getting pretty panicky in the Underworld. We'd always known that God would stoop to some pretty low tricks if it suited him but we never expected him to go as far as a full-blown incarnation. It's against all the rules of engagement – well, as far as we're concerned, anyway. Gods are allowed to become *like* human beings, just as long as they secretly hang on to all their powers tucked away up their tunic sleeves. But for God – *the* God – for him to become *genuinely* human is simply taking advantage. Devils can't do that, you see.

So when Jesus arrived on the scene – well, it got us rattled, I don't mind admitting. And when I was assigned to him I just knew I'd been given a tough nut to crack. So I decided to get some advice from lower down and I went to consult my under-viser.

'It's a great opportunity,' he reassured me. 'The arrogance of the Despicably Loving One will be his downfall. So he thinks he can make himself vulnerable to temptation and survive, does he? Choose your moment carefully, and don't forget what I always tell you: make it sound reasonable.'

I knew the moment had come when Jesus went into the

desert to pray: wanted to test his call, or find the direction of his mission or some other ghastly idea. I knew he'd be hungry, so I decided to home in on that. I pitched it very carefully – didn't want him to think of it as temptation, just pragmatism.

'You must be absolutely starving,' I said to him. 'You're the Son of God, aren't you, why not turn these stones into bread?'

'I don't need to,' he answered. 'The Bible says we don't just live on bread but on God's word.'

'Yeah, fine,' I countered, 'but it's a bit short on protein and carbohydrates, not to mention all those essential vitamins.' Well, the guy was supposed to know things no one else had yet discovered, so I might as well take advantage of that. Didn't seem to be working, though and I knew he was hungry.

'Okay, okay, so bread's boring; what about a triple-decker, double-whammy burger with crispy salad, extra relish and a mushroom-sauce topping – and you get a free plastic dinosaur to keep you company.'

I won't tell you what he said to that, but let's just say he wasn't impressed. Well, the first lesson you get taught in the Bachelor of Temptation seminars is not to pursue the same line too long. So I found another angle: I selected 'auto-suggestion' on the hand-held PC, chose 'cerebral cortex' in the destination box and clicked 'project'. I knew that his brain was now full of images of the wonders of the world. We'd chosen them very carefully: Egypt, India, China, Rome (of course) – all the great civilisations of the time. All this was now inside his head and all I had to do was get the sales pitch right.

'You could have the lot,' I murmured, seductively. 'All the power, all the prestige, not to mention the Ferrari in the garage . . . no one else will have one of those for ages, yet . . . and all you have to do is what I say. Just be a little flexible – compromise with the truth, grease the right palms, lick the right boots, and above all else, don't say anything you can't twist later to mean exactly the opposite.'

I really thought I'd got somewhere for a moment. I'd say he definitely weakened (even if HQ did tell me later that the instruments didn't even flicker), but he just said, 'The Bible says we should worship and serve only God – so why not push off you poor, puny little pipsqueak?'

I was gobsmacked – there'd never been anything said at training school about the Son of God using that sort of language, but later when I heard him having a go at the Pharisees I realised I'd got off lightly.

Time for another change of tack. Temptations are like wishes: we get to use them in threes (conservation of finite resources, you know) so I had to make the last one really good. I decided to do some research. Back to the palm-top, open 'mind-reader' and set the 'subject' box to 'nearest'. That should have been safe, since there was no one else within miles of us. Up it came on the screen, just like that – Satan help us all if this technology ever gets into mortals' hands – and I could see every word Jesus was thinking, at every level from the conscious right down to the subliminal.

'How do I draw people's attention – get them to listen to me?'

Of course! Back to the 'auto-suggestion' programme again (thank God for being so ridiculously open as to give us technology we can use against him) and after a couple of clicks I saw him look down and instinctively step backwards. Great! He was now on the uppermost pinnacle of a temple.

'Here's your gimmick,' I whispered. 'Jump off. You've been quoting the Bible at me, so let me remind you what it says. God will send an angel. He won't even allow you to hurt your foot. Go on, jump off and cause a sensation. They'll all listen to you after that.'

Jesus just said, 'The Bible says, don't put God to the test.' Short, but devastating. You could have knocked me over with a lock of Samson's hair (but that's another story). That line has always worked with religious people in the past; it's great because they can tell themselves they're 'doing it for the Lord' while *they* revel in all the glory. Why hadn't it worked? Well, there was no time to think about it, then – I had an appointment to keep at the Temple and I needed to go and recharge the hand-held before that.

Don't worry, though, I'll be back. I'm just biding my time, that's all.

PRAYING BIT

Temptation, Lord.
Oh dear, indeed.
Causes big problems.
Big scary ones that get in the way . . . of everything.

You seemed to be able to deal with it, though.
(Not really a surprise, I'll admit.)
And at least that tells me you do know what I'm going through.

But how did you do it?
How did you cope?
How come you never gave in?

I find it hard, Lord, almost impossible.
Some temptations just appear,
    others reappear – a lot.
And I don't like it.
And when I give in I feel dirty,
    even if I am forgiven.

You understand, don't you?
You know what I'm on about?
Like now, about that thing I did today?
I'm really sorry and I don't want to feel dirty.
Forgive me and wash away the grime.

Perhaps that's it, Lord;
    it's not necessarily temptation that's the problem.
It's the saying sorry and then accepting you're forgiven
    and then moving on that we find so hard.

Maybe that's why we keep falling down?

Amen.

Guess Who Came to Dinner?

Based on Luke 7:36-50

THINKING BIT

It's a disturbing thought, but Jesus wasn't really that at home in religious circles – the gospels show him much more at ease (and much more welcome) among the people who wouldn't darken the door even if they were allowed to. So where would Jesus be now?

I can only say that I've found him in churches – but he often hasn't been welcome there, and I've found him, too, in some places the Pharisees of the modern church wouldn't drive through in a bullet-proof car.

READING BIT

If I ever – and I mean ever – think of inviting Jesus to dinner again, do me a favour: bind me, gag me and lie me down in a darkened room until I recover.

I kid you not, it was the most embarrassing moment of my career as a Pharisee. I was having this party, and it was supposed to be a select affair with all the right people to be seen with. Then somebody whose opinion I used to respect said, 'Why not invite Jesus?'

Now, I'm not just being wise after the event – I said at the time I didn't think it was a good idea, but my friend's reasoning sounded persuasive.

'He's got the ear of the people,' he pointed out. 'If we get him on side now we'll be able to use him, bend him subtly to our ways. If not, he could be a real pain.'

Well, call me easily led if you like, but you must admit it's a plausible line. So I invited him, but I made it clear to all the staff: no fuss, and only the bare minimum of courtesies – 'we don't want to give the impression that he's one of us until he's shown he can fit in'.

Everything seemed okay at first. Jesus was obviously a well-brought-up sort of guy, from a respectable home. Why he'd wanted to leave all that to go on the road, I don't know. Anyway, he used the right knife and fork, swallowed his food before he drank and didn't talk with his mouth full, so I began to relax after a while – just too soon.

I don't know how that woman got in; the butler will pay for that mistake with his job, I promise you, but suddenly she was there, rushing over to Jesus and behaving in the most extraordinary way. I knew who she was – everyone in the district knew her, and quite a few of them knew her in the traditional biblical sense (none of my guests, I hasten to add). It was obvious she'd come to see Jesus, and that was why I didn't have her thrown out. I thought she might give him enough rope to hang himself with and for a while it looked as though she was doing just that.

If I hadn't thought it might serve my purpose I don't think I could have tolerated it – she rushed over to Jesus, blubbering like a brat and threw herself at his feet. He just sat there, with her filthy tears streaming all over his feet and watching her dry them with her hair. Then she got out this jar of myrrh (and there's only one way a woman like her could have afforded to buy myrrh) and poured it on his feet. Everybody was getting thoroughly embarrassed by this time, but I was secretly enjoying it. If this didn't drive a chariot and horses through his credibility, nothing would. After all, if he really was a prophet as people said, he would have known about her, even without her reputation to tell him. And letting her slobber all over him like that would have been unthinkable – ritual impurity and all that. So it was obvious he was a fake.

As I was thinking this, Jesus turned to me, with her still grovelling at his feet, and said, 'Simon, I've got something to ask you.'

Now I might be a pretty hot-shot lawyer, but if he thought I was going to get him out of the mess he was in, he was sadly mistaken, but I didn't say so of course.

'Ask away, *Teacher*,' I replied magnanimously with heavy irony.

'Well, there were these two debtors: one owed his creditor five hundred pounds, and the other fifty. Neither of them could pay, so he cancelled both the debts. Now, which would love him more for it?'

What was he up to? Why ask a lawyer a question like that?

Well, the answer was so obvious, and everyone was now looking at me, that I had to reply, hadn't I?

'The one who was let off the most, of course.'

'Right,' he said, and I thought I noticed an unsettling glint in his eye. 'See this woman, here?' (As if anyone could possibly not have noticed her!) 'When I got here you didn't offer me water to wash my feet – but she's used her own tears and her own hair. You didn't welcome me – a kiss would have been usual – but she's not stopped kissing my feet since she came in. And isn't it customary to offer an anointing of oil, as well? But she had to do that, too, because you couldn't be bothered.'

I really wondered where all this was leading. If he wanted all the social graces, then at least he could have run a comb through his own hair before he arrived. That's the trouble with these wandering preachers, they live rough, let their appearance go, make out it doesn't matter because they're 'spiritual', and then expect everyone else to make life civilised for them. Well, he'd picked the wrong guy here.

Then he went on. 'This woman has a lot to be forgiven for – and it's obvious she's experienced forgiveness because she's so full of love. Other people of course – mentioning no names because it's rude to embarrass one's host – don't think they need any forgiveness, so they're never open to it and don't experience it. I find people like that show very little love, don't you?'

Of course, I thought afterwards of all the things I ought to have said, but it was too late. But as it happened I didn't need to say anything, because he finally went too far. He turned to the woman and said, 'You're forgiven.'

So that's it! We'll use that against him one day. Meanwhile I'm going to be very careful whom I invite to my parties. 'You're forgiven,' indeed! Who, in heaven's name, does he think he is? God, or something?

PRAYING BIT

Lord,
    church can't half be dull.
I didn't used to go,
    and now I do,
    because I think I should.
That doesn't make it easier.

There are so many other things I'd rather do:
    like sleep in, walk the dog,
    or eat worms.

Sorry, that's not nice,
    but it's close to being true.
I'm told I can meet you there!
What? I meet you everywhere,
    and more often than not,
    when I'm *not* in church.

Like when I'm out shopping,
    or with friends,
    or just about to go to sleep.
You're everywhere, Lord,
    but church seems to be a bit of a barrier.

I'm not going to give up, Lord.
Going to church gives me a chance
    to meet others who chat to you; that's good.
And who knows,
    perhaps I'll be able to teach them something!

(Sorry to be cheeky, Lord.)

Amen.

Hold Your Head Up

Based on Luke 13:10-17

THINKING BIT

What was this 'spirit of infirmity' that had kept the woman bent double for eighteen years? Was it something spiritual, or physical? Or was it a 'demon' in the social and religious culture – the same one that still tells women to keep their heads down in some churches and not draw attention to themselves?

Why did Jesus say to her, not 'You are healed' but 'You are liberated'? Why did he give her the unusual title 'daughter of Abraham'?

You don't need to be a dedicated liberation theologian to see that there's a far greater miracle here than simply curing a bad back.

READING BIT

Abigail was a regular at the local synagogue. She knew all the rules and conventions and, most importantly, she knew 'her place'. She wasn't allowed to speak – with a voice like hers she'd have made a terrific reader, but even that was against the rules. She didn't know why – it was just the way things had always been done. So that meant it couldn't be changed.

So there she was, walking through the synagogue, trying not to draw attention to herself, when she saw this pair of feet. Nothing unusual in that; she'd learnt to keep her head down, so people's feet were all she generally saw when she was at worship. The trouble was that these feet were right in front of her, standing still and showing no sign of letting her past.

They were ordinary feet: touching the ground as feet do, most of the time; a bit rough around the toe-nails but clean enough. They'd been ritually washed at the door, no doubt, but they didn't look like the feet of a respectable religious person. These were the feet of a tramp, someone who spent his time walking from place to place. That was interesting – you didn't get many of those in your average congregation. Even so, she knew better than to look up. Eighteen years she'd been coming to this synagogue and never looked a man in the eye, yet – and she wasn't about to start now and get herself into grief with the authorities. She knew what they thought of women who drew attention to themselves, and she didn't want that kind of reputation, thank you very much.

She glanced left and right, but everywhere she looked there were more feet – no way of getting round these ones. Perhaps if she stood still he'd eventually notice her and move. No way. The feet just stayed there, the way feet do sometimes, and seemed to be challenging her to see who they belonged to.

'Oh, no,' she thought. 'I'm not falling for that one. Feet have been good enough for me for 18 years, and they can stay that way.'

Gradually, everything went quiet around her. People stopped walking around, hushed their voices, and you could have heard a thread fall from a prayer shawl it was so quiet. Have you ever been in that position – you just know that something's going on but you're afraid to look?

'Why are you bent like that? Have you hurt your back?'

Who was this, asking stupid questions? Before she could think what to say, Abbi felt a hand taking hold of hers. Yes, it definitely went with the feet: hard, roughened from the outdoor life, and definitely not well manicured. Okay, though.

Gradually, her hand was lifted up – not roughly as though she was about to be dragged outside or anything. In fact, there seemed to be something about it: kind and gentle, but not in a naff sort of a way. So it seemed somehow right to lift her head.

Yes, the face went with the feet, too. Didn't look as though that beard had seen a trimmer for a while, and the complexion had definitely been out in the sun too long. The guy might be poor, but is a comb too much to expect?

'That's better. Look everyone in the eye.'

What? Is this some kind of social radical or something?

He seemed to know what she was thinking. 'How does it feel to be liberated?'

That's it! Suddenly everything fell into place. There's only one thing worse than being oppressed: getting so used to it you don't notice any more. But, hey – the walls are actually more interesting than the floor, and at least *some* people's faces look better than their feet – and as for that ceiling – well, it's breathtaking.

What was really amazing was that they were all still there. The entire edifice of the synagogue hadn't crumbled to dust because a woman got noticed; people hadn't died of shock because she looked them in the eye.

One or two came close, mind you. Simon, the synagogue president, wasn't amused – well, he wouldn't be, would he?

'You can't do that,' he screeched hysterically. 'It's the sabbath! Healing counts as working.'

The man just gave him a look that had 'red herrings' written all over it. 'Irrelevant!' he answered. 'You'd pull a cow out of a ditch on the sabbath, wouldn't you? You'd water an ox on the sabbath.'

Simon was flummoxed at that – he thought the only things you had to water were cucumbers and geraniums – but he didn't get time to say it, which was probably a good thing because he was making enough of a fool of himself as it was.

'And here's this woman, a child of Abraham just like you, who's put up with eighteen years of petty-minded oppression. Eighteen years is bad enough, but you want to make it even longer by waiting for tomorrow?'

That did it. There was pandemonium in the precinct, consternation in the cloisters, conspiracy in the courtyard. Abbi's head was not only high but had now been well and truly filled with big ideas – like equality – and once that kind of thing happens, who knows where it will lead?

At last, the religious leaders were agreed about something: Jesus would have to go.

PRAYING BIT

It has to be said, Lord,
   you like to upset the norm.
I like that;
   it's exciting.
The norm?
Well, that's about as much fun
   as something that isn't.

OK, so it's only my opinion,
   but if the norm is wrong,
   then it really needs changing.

And that's what you did here, Lord.
In the most beautiful and gentle
   and powerful way.
No violence,
   no yelling,
   just a gentle, 'You can't be serious!'
And at a guess, that was followed by a little smile
   that said more than any speech.

Help me not to be normal, Lord.
I prefer the extremes.

Amen.

'Simon Says!'

Based on Luke 23:49-24:12, 34

THINKING BIT

Demon archaeologist Phyllis Stine has done it again: this fragment of a lost papyrus, a letter from Mary Magdalene, is claimed to be part of an exciting discovery: a collection of documents excavated in Alexandria, in an ancient clay pot with the inscription 'Philo's Facts' scratched into the clay.

Experts disagree on the authenticity, many claiming the document is an elaborate hoax and pointing out that there is nothing of significance in the fragment that could not have been gleaned from the existing evidence in the gospel according to Luke.

As to that, you must decide for yourselves – but either way, it certainly raises an issue about who were the first true 'apostles' (messengers) of the gospel of resurrection.

READING BIT

From Mary of Magdala to the overseers of the Christians in Jerusalem: Greetings.

I am writing to ask, yet again, why there isn't a woman on the board of apostles. If women are to play a proper role in any future community of faith, it seems to me to be important that someone asks that question. Perhaps it would be helpful if I reminded you all of the events of that amazing Passover weekend, and the role that my friends and I played.

When Jesus was dying on the cross, I was there, and so were the rest of us: the people always referred to as 'the women from Galilee'. Just for the record, they included Joanna and the other Mary – James' mother – and a few others as well whose names I don't recall. Anyway, the point is, we were there. I suppose it'll be difficult for people to understand what it felt like to stand and watch that happening. Plenty of times, soldiers and friends said, 'This is no place for women, why don't you go home?' In the event, it was a good thing we didn't, otherwise we'd never have known where the tomb was. That's my first point: we were there – even when it got dangerous; even though there was nothing we could do; even though it all seemed a pointless waste of time and tears, we were there.

When they took Jesus down from the cross, we followed at a safe distance to see where he was buried. We couldn't believe that after that ghastly death he was going to be dumped in a tomb with no burial rites. And why? Because of a religious festival that was considered more important than human dignity and pastoral care – talk about getting things out of proportion!

We knew we'd have to be discreet, so we met at first light on the Sunday, with spices to anoint the body. We hadn't a clue how we were going to get into the tomb, but sometimes if you try and cover all the angles first, you just end up doing nothing.

I don't mind admitting it was scary; the whole idea of going into a tomb in the semi-darkness gave me the jitters. And don't ask me to explain why we thought anointing a dead body was going to help: we just knew we had to do it – for our sake and for his mother's, if nothing else. As we approached, we saw that the stone had been rolled away. My first thought was that someone had come to do some further indignity to his body – nothing would surprise me – but we weren't just going to walk away and let it happen.

So we huddled a bit closer together and peered into the tomb. It was horrible – we couldn't see a thing at first and our imaginations just ran riot – real, creepy stuff – and we had to go right inside before our eyes could adjust and we began to see. We all braced ourselves for how Jesus would look – horribly mutilated, we knew, but we hadn't dared try to visualise it until now. Now we had to be prepared. I put my spice jar down and took hold of the hands either side of me. It seemed like hours we just stood there, staring into the darkness of the tomb, terrified of what we were about to see and wondering whether we'd have the courage to go through with it.

The darkness began to clear, and strange shadows played on the hewn-out walls of the tomb, a bit like the shadows you see in a darkened bedroom. We had to keep a real grip on ourselves, or our imaginations would probably have driven us completely mad. Gradually, the ghoulish images changed into contours in the rock, and we began to make out the shelf where the body would be. But slowly it dawned on us – it wasn't!

We were all completely at a loss! Where was Jesus? Had we got the wrong tomb? Had someone stolen the body? Then we had an even bigger shock. Suddenly, the place was full of light, and these two men appeared – dressed in glowing robes like I'd never seen before. We didn't see or hear them approach – they were just suddenly there. Now, I'm not speculating about who they were – I just tell what I see, and leave interpretation to people with less sense of danger. Anyway, while we were wondering what to do next, one of them spoke.

'Why look among the dead for someone who's alive?'

Alive! Now it was really getting spooky! But then as he went on I began to remember the things Jesus had said about new life, and about being killed and then raised again. And to be honest, nothing else made any sense, anyway. All in a rush, things fell into place, and we knew we were being told the truth. I've never seen Joanna run like it – except that time when a mouse came into her kitchen. Poor little beastie never stood a chance with Joanna after it, and it was trapped and despatched in no time.

Anyway, I digress. Mary and I took off after her and went to tell the news to you all. And did you believe us? Not a bit of it! 'Old wives' tales,' you said (who invented that saying, anyway?). We couldn't convince anyone; we were just silly women and what did we know! All day we tried, but you weren't having any of it. I suppose it would have ruined your street cred if you'd been caught listening to women's gossip!

Later on, Cleopas told me something that made me mad. He said that after he and Debs met Jesus at Emmaus, they came running back to tell you all about it. And what did someone say to them?

'We know it's true, because Simon says so.'

'Simon says', indeed! So when a *man* told you it suddenly all became credible, did it? Okay, I've made my point and I don't want to labour it. Look, I'm not interested in getting the credit, or saying, 'I told you so.' I just want to see that women like me get to play a full part in the Christian community. That's all.

Yours in his love,
Mary

PRAYING BIT

I often wonder what it was like, Lord,
    to go to the garden.
    and find an empty tomb.
Amazing.

Meeting those messengers
    must have been one of the most important meetings
    Mary ever had
    (short of actually meeting you, of course).

To be the first,
    the first to seek you
    and hear the Good News
    after all the hell of the weekend . . .

I'm in awe, Lord.
In awe of what Mary experienced,
    of what happened at that moment,
    and how it has affected the world since.

Mary was there, Lord.
That's important.
Perhaps we should all listen a little closer
    to people like her.

Amen.

Where There's a Well . . .

Based on John 4:3-42

THINKING BIT

Some of us can remember the time when for an Anglican to marry a 'non-conformist' would have been regarded by quite moderate, level-headed people as some kind of treason, surpassed only by actually crossing the divide oneself.

So, speaking as an Anglican, married to a Methodist, ordained as a Baptist and now a minister in the United Reformed Church, I'm glad those days have gone. Or have they? If they really had, there'd have been no need actually to change the labels, because it would be the content that mattered. Wouldn't it?

READING BIT

Hi, there – Sal's the name to my friends, but you can call me Sarah. Now, don't go getting all precious about it, we've only just met, haven't we? To be honest I shouldn't be talking to you at all – we're of different religions. I'm a Samaritan, you see, and to be absolutely candid, until I had my Life Transforming Experience I wouldn't have given you the time of day. Well, you get like that when everyone looks down on you because you're different.

Anyway, I've lived in Sychar all my life and never really questioned anything. It was just that everyone knew – or thought they did – that the Jews were a load of stuck-up snobs who thought they were better than everyone else. Yes, okay, but that's what I'd always been told I ought to believe.

So one day, there I was, going to the well (Jacob's well, actually) to draw water, and there was this guy sitting there. I didn't take much notice of him until he asked me to give him a drink, but as soon as he spoke I knew he was a Jew.

'Are you off your head?' I asked him. 'If your rabbi knew you were asking a Samaritan for a drink . . .'

'Well, please yourself,' he said – not at all unpleasantly. 'Then again, *you* could always ask *me* for a drink and I'd give you living water.'

Well, it was often said that the water in that well was alive, but somehow I didn't think that was what he meant. Not that I knew what he meant, but I had a shrewd idea it wasn't that.

I tried to cover up: 'Oh, sure, a well this deep, and you without a bucket. Where are you going to get this living water from, then? I suppose you think you're better than Jacob, do you? He gave us this well, after all.'

'That's true – and everyone who drinks from it will be thirsty again.'

Now, talk about stating the perishing obvious! But I didn't get the chance to interrupt him.

'If people drink the water I can give them, they'll never thirst again.'

Well, that sounded like an offer I couldn't refuse, especially with my feet the way the were, so I thought, fine! 'Well, what are you waiting for, then? Give me the water and save me all this bother every day.' I didn't have much confidence, though – the guy was talking in riddles, and I wasn't even sure he wasn't just a touch barking – until he said something else.

'Go and get your husband.'

'Well, since you ask, I haven't got one.'

'No, but you've had a few, though – five at the last count, I believe, and that doesn't include the chap you're living tally with at the moment.'

How by the prophet's ulcer did he know that? Perhaps he was somebody special after all. Well, if he was a holy man he could settle an argument for me.

'Look,' I said, 'all through our history we've worshipped on this mountain, but your lot say we should all go to Jerusalem. So who's right?'

'Oh, all that's going to be less important,' he replied. 'We're going to have to get used to worshipping wherever we can – and anyway, it's worshipping God in spirit and in truth that matters, and that's beginning to happen already.'

Now, that sounded like the start of a good conversation if

only his friends hadn't come back from their shopping trip at that moment and started getting sniffy about the fact that he was talking to me. Oh, they didn't actually say anything – but it was pretty obvious how they felt. Mind you, that's something I've noticed since I got to know him – Jesus is a lot more approachable than his friends are. (Did I tell you that that was who it was, by the way? Well, you must have guessed, anyway.) I decided not to hang around but go and get my neighbours. So I hot-footed it back into the town to find them.

At first, no one really believed me. I'm not surprised, because if I'm honest, my lot are just as prejudiced as any other.

'What? One of that Jerusalem lot?'

'The ones who worship oddly?'

'And think they're the only ones that are right?'

'That's funny,' I said. 'Isn't that what they say about us?' That got them going again.

'Our worship's not odd – it's imaginative.'

'And we *are* right.'

I decided a change of tack was needed. 'He told me all about myself – and he's never met me before.' I knew that would get them interested; give them something they can't explain and they're shouting 'prophet' before you finish the sentence.

Anyway, they came with me and met Jesus. And they liked him. And they asked him to stay.

Amazingly, some of them aren't quite so sure any more that they're right. Not that that means they think the other lot are, mind you.

But some of us are getting to think that *he* is.

PRAYING BIT

People say religion causes loads of problems.
(Oh, hi, Lord.)
They're right; it does.
Or is at least used as an excuse.

But what amazes me
    is how it's used against itself.
I mean, Lord, what's going on here?
Why do we care about labels?
Why can't we just move on
    and accept that we all differ?

And if it's OK to stick my neck out a bit,
    I bet you don't really care that much.
I bet you're not fussed how people get baptised,
    how they have communion,
        whether they're Roman Catholic or C of E,
        or if they dress nicely for morning worship.

None of that's important.
You said so.
You said so a lot.

Perhaps it's about time we started listening
    and instead of blaming,
        be slow to criticise others
        and quick to help them.

That makes much more sense.

Amen.

You Just Don't See It, Do You?

Based on John 9

THINKING BIT

There's none so blind as those that will not see. Okay, okay, so it's cliché time. Alright, then, try this one.

Someone asked Helen Keller if she could think of anything worse than being blind. 'Yes,' she replied. 'Being sighted, but having no vision.'

Get it? Well I should jolly well hope so – even Gatward didn't need that one explaining to him, so it can't be that difficult.

READING BIT

Look, I don't know how many times I have to say this – you Pharisees are more blind than I used to be – Jesus healed me, and he's okay. Okay?

I don't know who's worse, you or those friends of his who were asking whose sin had caused my blindness. The same old story – blame the victim. And now that he's healed me you lot are out to get him because you can't stand being upstaged by someone who doesn't talk posh and hasn't got a degree in philosophy. It's simple enough: once I was blind, now I can see; end of story.

Alright, then: beginning of story. But this is the last time I'm telling it other than to a journalist with a fat cheque book. Understand?

I was sitting at the side of the road begging, the way you do – well, the way I used to do, anyway – when I heard these people talking. I'd heard it all before, or thought I had, so I didn't take much notice at first. It was only later I realised it was Jesus and his friends. Well, they started off by asking him the usual silly question – as though any kind of disability always has to be someone's fault. Oh, and before anyone starts any other silly rumours: no, I wasn't paying for sins I'd committed in a previous life, either. Jesus said something about showing God's glory, and about his being the light of the world – strange stuff, really, but I suppose we might all understand it one day – and then I heard someone spit. Well, you get a lot of that sort of thing when you're begging, and I've given up complaining about it now – it only encourages them.

This was different, though. Suddenly, I felt all this sticky stuff being put onto my eyes. It didn't take a rabbinical school education to work out what was going on, and I wasn't impressed, but before I had a chance to say so, he told me to go and wash it off. Well, I didn't need any second bidding, I can tell you. So off I went to the pool of Siloam and scrubbed like never before.

(Are you with me so far? It's just that I know you Pharisees sometimes find it hard to concentrate on the truth, know what I mean? Good.)

Well, no sooner had I dried my eyes than I started to make out shapes, all different sorts and sizes. Gradually they got clearer and I got my first glimpse of current Jerusalem fashions – being able to see is obviously a mixed blessing: in more ways than one, too. As soon as people realised I could see, they were all over me, trying to get back the money I'd begged from them and accusing me of being a con merchant. So I ended up being dragged up in front of you lot and given the third degree.

Oh you just had to find someone to get at, didn't you! If it wasn't me for being a liar, it was Jesus for working on the Sabbath. I don't care what you say – he's a good bloke, he is, and he's got a sight more of God in him than all of you lot put together.

But you weren't satisfied with my word, were you – had to go and drag my parents into it and ask them if I'd really been blind. I don't blame them for being evasive; they know what you people are capable of. They know it's instant excommunication to disagree with you and that's why they told you to ask me. So next thing I knew, I was up in front of you again with all of you yelling at me that Jesus was a bad man and trying to put words into my mouth that were a sight less appetising than what he'd put on my eyes.

All of this is doing my head in! You used to say that I was blind, and I was, but I can recognise a good man when he's standing in front of me. And I don't see any at this precise moment.

It's no use you getting all blustery with me – I've been on the streets all my life, remember – I can look after myself, and I'm not going to be intimidated by you. Okay, so you're going to ban me from your rotten synagogue – well that's fine. I've never been able to join in anything in my life before so what's different?

Look, it's as plain as the nose on your face – and in some cases nothing comes any plainer. I was blind. Now I see. Finito.

What?

Oh, don't go over all that again. I've already told you once what he did to me, and you didn't listen then, so don't waste my time with your pathetic games. What d'you want to hear it again for – unless you're thinking of joining his disciples yourselves.

You what? 'Disciples of Moses'? What's that supposed to mean? Well, there's a turn up! You clever space-wasters say you don't know where Jesus is from? Well, he opened my eyes, which is more than he's ever likely to be able to do for you – so it's pretty obvious, isn't it?

He's from God. You know, the Unmentionable Great One, blessed be he – the one you're supposed to be so pally with? If he wasn't from God, he wouldn't be going around doing this sort of thing, would he?

Yeah, I know, I've heard all the stock clichés before. I was 'born into sin' – well, if that were true, it wouldn't be my fault, would it – what's your excuse?

Oh, don't worry, I'm going. I'm not fooled by your little games. After all, I came in here with my eyes wide open, and I'm going out the same way. You ought to try it sometime.

PRAYING BIT

Born into sin?
Lord, that sounds crazy.
I know there's an argument somewhere
    about something,
        (you can tell I really understand it)
        but it does sound mad.

Am I wrong? Out of order?
I dunno.
I just don't like the notion that we're born to it.
I guess humanity as a whole
    is responsible for some of the rubbish,
    but that's different from blame.

Compare me to a new-born;
    or a twenty-something
    to a four-year-old.
Seems to me that's pretty unfair.
Because if we're born to it,
    who's actually to blame?
No one by the sound of it.

We grow into sin
    because we're human and full of failures.
But you love us and help us.
Perhaps we should concentrate on that
    a bit more instead?

Amen.

BY THE SAME AUTHORS

GET REAL GOD!

A SORT OF BIBLE STUDY BOOK FOR TEENAGERS

MICHAEL FORSTER
DAVID GATWARD

ISBN 1 84003 099 2
Catalogue No 1500159

Occasionally a book comes along that smashes through tradition and changes the way things are done for ever. Is *this* that book? *Get Real!* Of course it is! But we would say that, wouldn't we?

Inside you'll find an entirely new approach to reading the Bible and learning from it. But rather than tell you about it here, why not take a look for yourself?

Go on – get real with God!